POOR WOMEN, POOR CHILDREN

American Poverty in the 1990s

HARRELL R. RODGERS, Jr.

Third
Edition

M.E. Sharpe
Armonk, New York
London, England

Library of Congress Cataloging-in-Publication Data

Rodgers, Harrell R.
Poor women, poor children : American poverty in
the 1990s / by Harrell R. Rodgers, Jr. — 3rd ed.
p.   cm.
Rev. ed. of: Poor women, poor families.
Rev. ed. © 1990.
Includes bibliographical references and index.
ISBN 1-56324-607-4 (alk. paper). —
ISBN 1-56324-608-2 (pbk. : alk. paper)
1. Women heads of households—United States.
2. Poor women—United States.
3. Women—Employment—United States.
4. Public welfare—United States.
I. Rodgers, Harrell R. Poor women, poor families.
II. Title.
HV1445.R64   1996
362.83′0973—dc20   95-41481

CIP

Printed in the United States of America

The paper used in this publication meets the minimum requirements of
American National Standard for Information Sciences—
Permanence of Paper for Printed Library Materials,
ANSI Z 39.48-1984.

BM (c)   10   9   8   7   6   5   4   3   2   1
BM (p)   10   9   8   7   6   5   4   3

Contents

List of Tables and Figures

Tables

Figures

Acknowledgments

In writing the third edition of this book I entertained the perfectly absurd notion on more than one occasion that the entire U.S. Congress was engaged in a conspiracy to thwart my efforts. Congress spent most of 1995 seriously debating and rewriting various versions of a major overhaul of welfare, announcing one completion date after another. As I wrote and rewrote along with them, 1995 came to an end with no agreement between Congress and the president on reform. For the most part unhampered by Congress, more than half the states adopted major welfare reform plans, while most of the other states are debating major innovations. Thus, this edition was written during a period of change in welfare policy unprecedented since the 1960s. I have endeavored throughout the book to capture this mood and the thrust and implications of the changes taking place.

As in writing the previous editions of this book, I have been blessed with an excellent base of academic literature and considerable personal assistance. Jean Tash, statistical assistant, at the Bureau of the Census was always inspired and tireless in helping me track down unpublished data and obtain assistance from other researchers within the Departments of Commerce and Health and Human Services. Gordon Fisher, at the Office of the Assistant

Secretary for Planning and Evaluation, provided invaluable insights into the origins and development of the federal poverty standards and also directed me to other valuable research. Glenn Phillips, with the staff of the House Ways and Means Committee, took time out of a frantic schedule on more than one occasion to help me locate much-needed data and information. To each my warmest thanks.

The crew at M.E. Sharpe was, as usual, wonderful. Patricia Kolb, executive editor, encouraged me to undertake this edition and organized my efforts. Her assistant, Elizabeth T. Granda, served as the communication specialist to keep the working team in contact. Eileen M. Gaffney, production editor, did the hard work. She directed the editing, artwork, and printing and saw that the project was finished. To each my continuing thanks and admiration.

Henry Trueba, senior vice president and provost, Richard Rozelle, dean of social sciences, and Kent Tedin, chair of political science, at the University of Houston combined their efforts to provide me with time off to write this book. I am most grateful for their kindness and support.

I am blessed with a wonderful partner in my wife, Lynne. This year she took time out of her own busy schedule to give birth to Michael James. With all my love, this book is dedicated to Michael and his truly wonderful mother.

POOR WOMEN, POOR CHILDREN

Chapter 1

The Increasing Numbers
of Poor Women and Children

It is up to us to determine whether the years ahead
will be for humankind a curse or a blessing.
—Elie Wiesel

Poverty continues to be one of America's most serious social
problems. Despite the fact that America may be the richest
nation in the world, a substantial proportion of the American
population lives in poverty. In 1993 the federal government
counted 39.3 million Americans living below the poverty line,
about 15 percent of the population (Bureau of the Census
1995, xvi). This is a huge number of people. Fewer than 30
million people live in all of Canada. The American poverty
population is, in fact, larger than the combined total populations of Maine, New Hampshire, Vermont, Massachusetts,
Rhode Island, Connecticut, Iowa, North Dakota, South Dakota,
Nebraska, Delaware, West Virginia, Montana, Idaho, Wyo-
ming, Colorado, New Mexico, Arizona, Utah, Nevada, Alaska,
and Hawaii.

Poverty has increased in recent years and has proven an extremely difficult problem to ameliorate, in significant part because one of the most vulnerable groups—mother-only families—has grown very rapidly over the last thirty years as a proportion of all families. Between 1970 and 1993 the number of mother-only families with children more than doubled, from 3.8 million to 8.7 million (Figure 1.1). During this same period, the number of two-parent families with children increased by only 1.3 percent. As a consequence of these changes, by 1993 almost one of every four American families with children was headed by a woman, compared to one in ten in 1960 (Bureau of the Census 1995, D22).

As Table 1.1 (p. 6) shows, in 1960 only 8 percent of all children under eighteen lived in a family headed by a single woman. In 1993 the percentage was almost one in four, 23.3 percent, including some 17 percent of white children, 28 percent of Hispanic children, and a majority, 54 percent, of all black children (Figure 1.2 [p. 7]). The number of children in single-parent families has increased dramatically. In 1993 some 17.9 million children lived with only one parent, 87 percent of those—over 15 million—with their mother. In 1960 a third of that number, about 5 million children, lived in mother-only families (Table 1.1). Of the current generation of all American children, more than half will spend some of their childhood in a household headed by a single mother (Sweet and Bumpass 1987; Bumpass and Raley 1993). A significant percentage will spend their entire childhood in a mother-only family.

Single mothers and their dependent children are extremely vulnerable economically, educationally, and socially. These families suffer extremely high rates of poverty. In 1993 over 46 percent of all families with children headed by a single woman lived in poverty. By contrast, only 9 percent of all married-couple families with dependent children had incomes below the poverty level (U.S. House 1994, 1161; Bureau of the Census 1995, D22). Eleven percent of the mother-only families were poor despite the fact that the mother worked full-time year-round.

Figure 1.1. Mother-Only Families with Children, 1959–1993

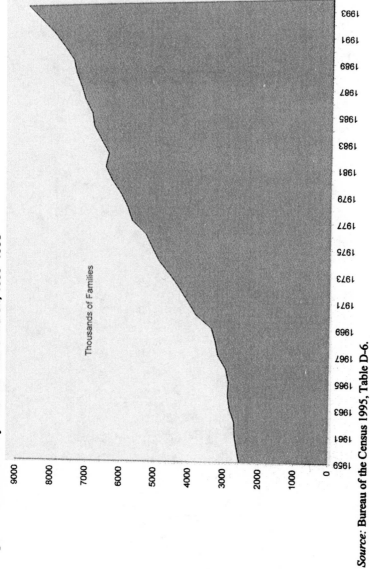

Thousands of Families

Source: Bureau of the Census 1995, Table D-6.

Table 1.1

Living Arrangements of Children Under 18, 1960 and 1993

	All races		White		Black		Hispanic	
	1960	1993	1960	1993	1960	1993	1980	1993
Total number of children	63,727	66,893	55,077	53,075	8,650	10,660	5,459	7,776
living with								
Two parents	55,877 (87.7)	47,181 (70.5)	50,082 (90.9)	40,996 (77.2)	5,795 (67.0)	3,796 (35.6)	4,116 (75.4)	5,017 (64.5)
One parent	5,829 (9.1)	17,872 (26.7)	3,932 (7.1)	11,110 (20.9)	1,897 (20.9)	6,079 (57.0)	1,152 (21.1)	2,472 (31.8)
Mother only	5,105 (8.0)	15,586 (23.3)	3,381 (6.1)	9,256 (17.4)	1,723 (19.9)	5,757 (54.0)	1,069 (19.6)	2,176 (28.0)
Father only	724 (1.1)	2,286 (3.4)	551 (1.0)	1,854 (3.3)	173 (2.0)	322 (3.0)	83 (1.5)	296 (3.8)
Other relative or nonrelative	2,021 (3.2)	1,841 (2.8)	1,062 (1.9)	969 (1.9)	959 (11.1)	784 (8.4)	191 (3.5)	286 (3.6)

Source: U.S. House 1994 (*Green Book*): 1113–1116.
Note: Numbers may not sum due to rounding.

Figure 1.2. Living Arrangements of Children, 1993

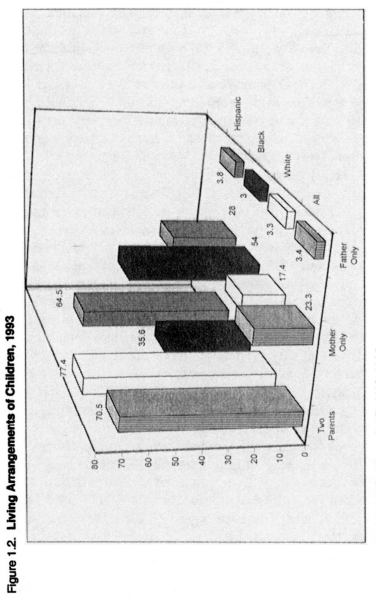

Source: U.S. House 1994 (*Green Book*): 1113–1116.

There are basically five reasons why mother-only families are so poor: (1) on average women still have less earning potential than men; (2) single women with dependent children have very high unemployment rates; (3) unlike married-couple families, which often have two employed adults, mother-only families have fewer earners; (4) most of these families receive either no support from absent fathers or inadequate support; and (5) American public policies have not been revised in light of the massive changes in family demographics described here.

The majority of mother-only families today are the consequence of divorce and separation, and a small percentage (around 4%) result from mothers' being widowed (Figure 1.3). In 1960 only about 1 percent of all children under eighteen experienced parental divorce (Table 1.2 [p. 10]). Today the figure is closer to half. Additionally, an increasingly large proportion of mother-only families are the outcome of births to unwed women. In 1970 only about 7 percent of all mother-only families were the product of out-of-wedlock births. By 1993 the figure was about 36 percent. In recent years almost 30 percent of all children have been born out of wedlock, up from 5 percent in 1960. Birthrates among unwed women increased by more than 70 percent between 1983 and 1993 alone. The rate was particularly high for black mother-only families. In 1970 about one in six black mother-only families was the result of out-of-wedlock births. In 1993 the rate was three in five. Unwed mothers have the highest poverty rate of any family type, have very modest average incomes from all sources, and tend to suffer the longest stays on welfare. Yet these families are becoming increasingly common.

Why do we have so many more female-headed households today than in the past? A number of explanations have been advanced and will be examined more thoroughly in the chapters that follow. It is often argued (Wilson 1987) that many young men, especially black men, do not marry because increasingly they cannot find jobs that pay well enough to support a family. Another explanation is that changing social values make it more acceptable for women to have children

Figure 1.3. Living Arrangements of Children in Mother-Only Families, 1993

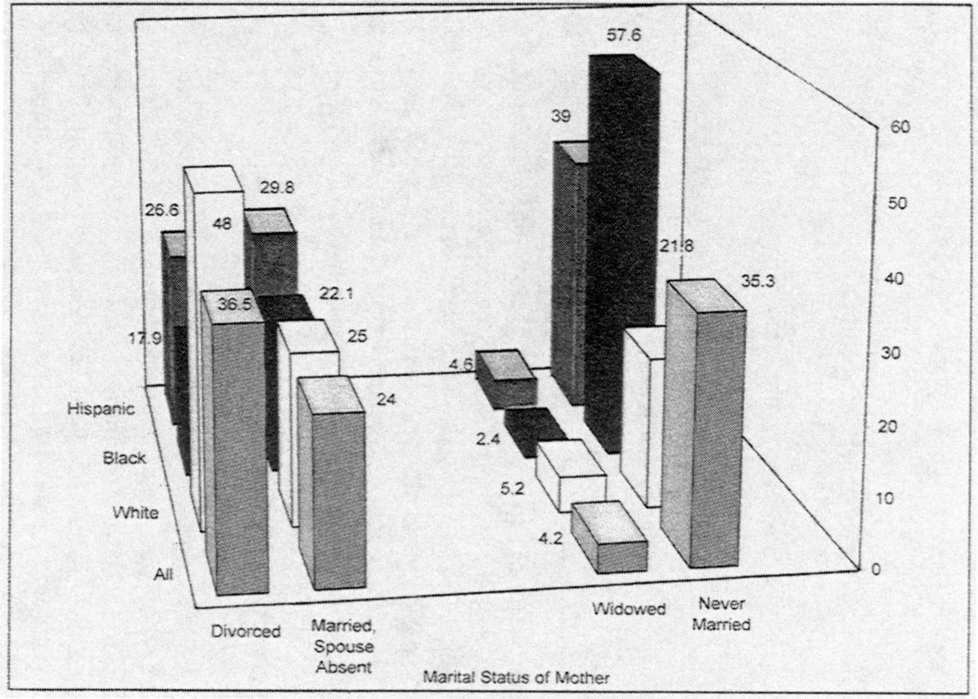

Source: Bureau of the Census 1994b, p. vi.

Table 1.2

The State of Children

1960		1990
5%	Children born to unmarried mothers	28%
7%	Children under three living with one parent	27%
Less than 1%	Children under 18 experiencing the divorce of their parents	Almost 50%
17%	Mothers returning to work within one year of a child's birth	53%
18.6%	Married women in labor force with children under 6 years old	60%
10%	Children under 18 living in a one-parent family	27%
27%	Children under 18 living below the poverty line	22.7%

Source: Carnegie Corporation Report 1994, 11.

out of wedlock. It is also noted that increased rates of divorce may be related to improved employment and career options for women, allowing them to be more independent. Finally, the evidence suggests that expansion of welfare programs since the 1960s may make it easier for women to head households (Gottschalk, McLanahan, and Sandefur 1994).

Poverty Among Children

One of the most ominous consequences of increases in the number of poor mother-only families is the deprivation brought to their dependent children. As more and more mother-only families have fallen below the poverty level, poverty rates among children that were once declining have reversed and are now increasing significantly. Considerable progress was made in reducing child poverty between 1966 and 1979, but since 1981 poverty among children has averaged over 20 percent. As Table 1.3 (pp. 12–13) and Figure 1.4 (p. 14) show, the rate of poverty was considerably higher for children of all races in 1993 than in 1976.

The number of poor children is daunting. In 1993 there were almost 16 million poor children of all races in all family types (Table 1.3). This is almost as many as the population of Texas. Numerically the majority of all poor children are white, but the poverty rate is considerably higher for minority children. Minority children have long suffered a particularly high rate of poverty, and poverty rates for white children have increased significantly since 1980. In 1993, 22.7 percent of all American children were poor. This included 17.8 percent of all white children, 40.9 percent of all children of Hispanic origin, and 46 percent of all black children (Figure 1.5). Poverty rates among children under six are even higher. In 1993 almost 26 percent of all children under six lived in poverty (U.S. House 1994, 1151).

Tragically, these figures reveal that children are the poorest age group in America. Where poverty is concerned, it is a great deal safer to be old than young in America. As we will detail in chapter 5, American children suffer a much higher rate of poverty than children in other Western industrial nations.

More than half of all the poor children in America now live in mother-only families, compared with only 25 percent in the late 1950s and early 1960s (U.S. House 1994, 1149; Bureau of the Census 1995, 22). As Table 1.4 (pp. 16–17) shows, in 1993 there were 8.5 million related poor children living in female-headed families (57% of all poor children), almost double the 4.3 million in the mid-1960s. By contrast, there were 7.9 million related poor children in families with an adult male present in 1966 (65% of all poor children), but 5.8 million in families of this type in 1993 (43%). (See Figures 1.4 and 1.6 [pp. 14, 18] for breakdown by race of all poor children in mother-only families.)

To be a child in a mother-only family is to suffer enormous economic risks. Over half of all the children who live in mother-only families exist below the poverty line (Table 1.5 [p. 19] and Figure 1.7 [p. 20]). By comparison, the poverty rate for children

Table 1.3

Poor Children by Race, 1974–1993 (in thousands)

	Total	Black	White	Hispanic[a]
1974	10,156	3,755	6,223	NA
1975	11,104	3,925	6,927	NA
1976	10,273	3,787	6,189	1,443
1977	10,288	3,888	6,097	1,422
1978	9,931	3,830	5,831	1,384
1979	10,377	3,833	6,193	1,535
1980	11,543	3,961	7,181	1,749
1981	12,505	4,237	7,785	1,925
1982	13,647	4,472	8,678	2,181
1983	13,911	4,398	8,862	2,312
1984	13,420	4,413	8,472	2,376
1985	13,010	4,157	8,253	2,606
1986	12,876	4,148	8,209	2,507
1987[b]	12,843	4,385	7,788	2,670
1988	12,455	4,296	7,435	2,631
1989	12,590	4,375	7,599	2,603
1990	13,431	4,550	8,232	2,865
1991	14,341	4,755	8,848	3,094
1992	14,617	4,938	8,955	3,116
1993	15,727	5,125	9,752	3,873

		Percentage composition		
1974		37.0	61.3	NA
1976		36.9	60.2	14.0
1980		34.3	62.2	15.2
1984		32.9	63.1	17.7
1988		34.5	59.7	21.1
1990		33.9	62.0	21.2
1991		33.2	61.7	21.6
1992		33.8	61.3	21.3
1993		32.6	62.0	24.6

		Rates		
1974	15.4	39.8	11.2	NA
1975	17.1	41.7	12.7	NA
1976	16.0	40.6	11.6	30.2
1977	16.2	41.8	11.6	28.3
1978	15.9	41.5	11.3	27.6
1979	16.4	41.2	11.8	28.0
1980	18.3	42.3	13.9	33.2
1981	20.0	45.2	15.2	35.8
1982	21.9	47.6	17.0	39.4
1983	22.3	46.7	17.5	38.1

1984	21.5	46.5	16.7	39.2
1985	20.7	43.6	16.2	40.3
1986	20.5	43.1	16.1	37.7
1987[b]	20.3	45.1	15.3	39.3
1988	19.5	43.5	14.5	37.6
1989	19.6	43.7	14.8	36.2
1990	20.6	44.8	15.9	38.4
1991	21.8	45.9	16.8	40.4
1992	21.9	46.6	16.9	39.9
1993	22.7	46.1	17.8	40.9

Sources: Bureau of the Census 1993, Table 3; U.S. House 1994 (*Green Book*): 1148; Bureau of the Census 1995, Table C.

Note: Includes all persons under 18 below the poverty level, including unrelated children.

[a]Hispanic origin may be of any race; this category is not exclusive.

[b]The 1987 numbers have not been revised.

NA: Not available.

---

in families with an adult male is less than 12 percent. In mother-only families the poverty rate for white children is high (over 45.6%), but lower than the rate for black (65.9%) and Hispanic (66.1%) families. About 75 percent of children in mother-only families live either in poverty or rather close to the poverty level (Bureau of the Census 1995, 22). A congressional study in 1985 estimated that if "the proportion of children in female-headed families had not increased during the past 25 years, . . . the number of poor children in 1983 might have been . . . 22 percent lower" (U.S. House 1985a, 7). A 22 percent reduction in the current rate of poverty among children would lower the number of poor children by about 3 million.

The Impact of Poverty on Children

Most of the children who experience poverty, including those who spend a significant portion of their childhood years in a poor family, will survive the experience. Most will go on to graduate from high school, find employment, and raise a family. Still, the evidence documents that children who grow up in poverty are twice as likely to drop out of school and one and a half times as likely to be unemployed, while the girls are four

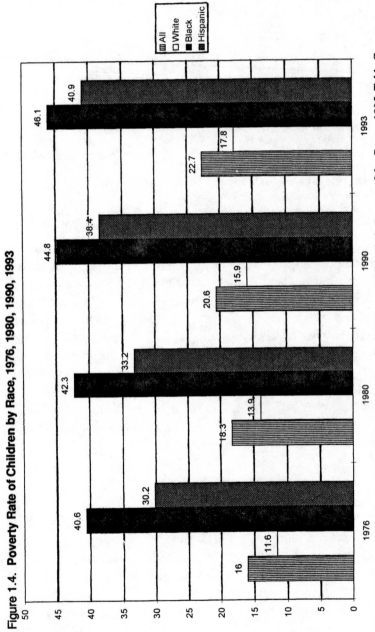

Figure 1.4. Poverty Rate of Children by Race, 1976, 1980, 1990, 1993

Source: Bureau of the Census 1993, Table 3; U.S. House 1994 (*Green Book*): 1148; Bureau of the Census 1995, Table C.

Figure 1.5. Poor Children, 1993

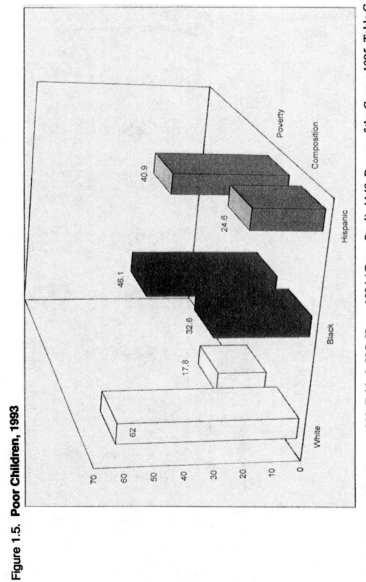

Source: Bureau of the Census 1993, Table 3; U.S. House 1994 (*Green Book*): 1148; Bureau of the Census 1995, Table C.
Note: Hispanics may be of any race. This is an overlapping category.

Table 1.4

Poverty Among Related Children in Families, 1966–1993 (in thousands)

Year	Total poor	Female head					Male present				
		Nonwhite	White	Hispanic[a]	Total	Percentage of total	Nonwhite	White	Hispanic[a]	Total	Percentage of total
1966	12,146	2,150	2,112	NA	4,262	35.1	2,792	5,092	NA	7,884	64.9
1967	11,427	2,316	1,930	NA	4,246	37.2	2,382	4,799	NA	7,181	62.8
1968	10,739	2,334	2,075	NA	4,409	41.1	2,032	4,298	NA	6,330	58.9
1969	9,500	2,179	2,068	NA	4,247	44.7	1,655	3,598	NA	5,253	55.3
1970	10,235	2,442	2,247	NA	4,689	45.8	1,651	3,891	NA	5,542	54.2
1971	10,344	2,398	2,452	NA	4,850	46.9	1,605	3,889	NA	5,494	53.1
1972	10,082	2,821	2,273	NA	5,094	50.5	1,477	3,511	NA	4,988	49.5
1973	9,453	2,710	2,461	606	5,171	54.7	1,281	3,001	758	4,282	45.3
1974	9,966	2,678	2,683	621	5,361	53.8	1,209	3,396	793	4,605	46.2
1975	10,881	2,784	2,813	694	5,597	51.4	1,350	3,394	925	5,284	48.6
1976	10,080	2,870	2,713	636	5,583	55.4	1,176	3,321	789	4,497	44.6
1977	10,029	2,965	2,693	686	5,658	56.4	1,121	3,250	716	4,371	43.6
1978	9,722	3,060	2,627	663	5,687	58.5	988	3,047	692	4,035	41.5
1979	9,933	3,006	2,629	668	5,635	56.4	1,079	3,279	837	4,358	43.6
1980	11,114	3,053	2,813	809	5,866	52.8	1,244	4,004	909	5,248	47.2

1981	12,069	3,185	3,120	909	6,305	52.2	1,455	4,309	966	5,764	47.8
1982	13,139	3,447	3,249	990	6,696	51.0	1,411	5,032	1,127	6,443	49.0
1983	13,427	3,359	3,388	1,018	6,747	50.2	1,534	5,146	1,233	6,680	49.8
1984	12,929	3,395	3,377	1,093	6,772	52.4	1,448	4,709	1,223	6,157	47.6
1985	12,483	3,344	3,372	1,247	6,716	53.8	1,300	4,467	1,266	5,767	46.2
1986	12,257	3,421	3,522	1,194	6,943	56.6	1,121	4,192	1,219	5,313	43.3
1987	12,435	3,600	3,474	1,241	7,074	56.9	1,285	4,076	1,390	5,361	43.1
1987[b]	12,275	3,586	3,433	1,250	7,019	57.2	1,291	3,966	1,356	5,257	42.8
1988	11,935	3,530	3,424	1,294	6,954	58.3	1,310	3,671	1,282	4,981	41.7
1989	12,001	3,553	3,255	1,158	6,808	56.7	1,285	3,908	1,338	5,193	43.3
1990	12,715	3,766	3,597	1,314	7,363	57.9	1,253	4,098	1,437	5,352	42.1
1991	13,658	4,125	3,941	1,398	8,065	59.1	1,217	4,376	1,579	5,593	40.9
1992	13,876	4,250	3,783	1,289	8,032	57.9	1,293	4,550	1,657	5,844	42.1
1993	14,961	4,104	4,102	1,673	8,503	56.8	765	4,615	1,872	5,845	43.2

Sources: Bureau of the Census 1988a; figures for 1987 (revised) to 1992 are from *Current Population Survey* (CPS) (March of each year); U.S. House 1994 (*Green Book*): 1149; Bureau of the Census 1995, Table 8. Table prepared by Congressional Research Service.

Notes: Includes only related children in families. Estimates for 1987 (revised) through 1991 are not comparable to prior years due to processing changes in the CPS. Numbers may not sum due to rounding.

[a]Persons of Hispanic origin may be of any race.

[b]Revised.

NA: Not available.

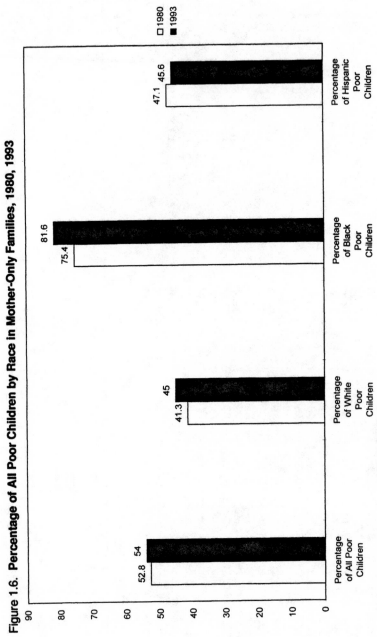

Figure 1.6. Percentage of All Poor Children by Race in Mother-Only Families, 1980, 1993

□1980
■1993

Percentage of Hispanic Poor Children: 47.1 (1980), 45.6 (1993)

Percentage of Black Poor Children: 75.4 (1980), 81.6 (1993)

Percentage of White Poor Children: 41.3 (1980), 45 (1993)

Percentage of All Poor Children: 52.8 (1980), 54 (1993)

Source: Bureau of the Census 1995, Table D-6.

Table 1.5

Poverty Rate of Children by Family Type and Race, 1966–1993

Year	Total	Female head				Male present			
		Black	White	Hispanic	Total	Black	White	Hispanic	Total
1966	17.4	76.6	46.9	NA	58.2	39.9	9.2	NA	12.6
1967	16.3	72.4	42.1	NA	54.3	35.3	8.7	NA	11.5
1968	15.3	70.5	44.4	NA	55.2	29.8	7.8	NA	10.2
1969	13.8	68.2	45.2	NA	54.4	25.0	6.7	NA	8.6
1970	14.9	67.7	43.1	NA	53.0	26.0	7.3	NA	9.2
1971	15.1	66.6	44.6	NA	53.1	25.5	7.4	NA	9.3
1972	14.9	69.5	41.1	NA	53.1	24.1	6.8	NA	8.6
1973	14.2	67.2	42.1	68.7	52.1	21.7	6.0	18.8	7.6
1974	15.1	65.0	42.9	64.3	51.5	20.0	6.9	20.0	8.7
1975	16.8	66.0	44.2	68.4	52.7	22.1	8.2	23.8	9.8
1976	15.8	65.6	42.7	67.3	52.0	19.4	7.1	20.8	8.5
1977	16.0	65.7	40.3	68.6	50.3	19.9	7.1	17.9	8.5
1978	15.7	66.4	39.9	68.9	50.6	17.6	6.8	17.2	7.9
1979	16.0	63.1	38.6	62.2	48.6	18.7	7.3	19.2	8.5
1980	17.9	64.8	41.6	65.0	50.8	20.3	9.0	22.9	10.4
1981	19.5	67.7	42.8	67.3	52.3	23.4	10.0	24.5	11.6
1982	21.3	70.7	46.5	71.8	56.0	24.1	11.6	27.8	13.0
1983	21.8	68.3	47.1	70.6	55.4	23.7	12.0	27.2	13.5
1984	21.0	66.2	45.9	71.0	54.0	24.3	11.0	27.5	12.5
1985	20.1	66.9	45.2	72.4	53.6	18.8	10.4	27.4	11.7
1986	19.8	67.1	46.3	66.7	54.4	17.0	9.8	25.8	10.8
1987	20.0	68.3	45.8	70.1	54.7	19.8	9.5	28.3	10.9
1987[a]	19.7	66.9	45.0	69.8	53.7	19.1	9.3	27.7	10.6
1988	19.0	64.7	44.9	69.6	52.9	18.7	8.5	25.4	10.0
1989	19.0	63.1	42.5	64.3	51.1	20.3	9.1	25.5	10.4
1990	19.9	64.7	45.9	68.4	53.4	19.3	9.5	26.7	10.7
1991	21.1	68.2	47.1	68.6	55.5	17.3	10.1	29.1	11.1
1992	21.1	67.1	45.3	65.7	54.3	19.4	10.4	29.5	11.5
1993	22.7	65.9	45.6	66.1	53.7	18.0	10.8	30.1	11.7

Source: Bureau of the Census 1988a; figures for 1987 (revised) through 1993 are from March *Current Population Survey;* U.S. House 1994 (*Green Book*): 1150. Table prepared by Congressional Research Service.

Note: Persons of Hispanic origin may be of any race.

[a]Revised.

NA: Not available.

times as likely to become an unwed mother (Gottschalk, McLanahan, and Sandefur 1994, 102; Blankenhorn 1994). Children who suffer long-term poverty are much more likely to suffer

20

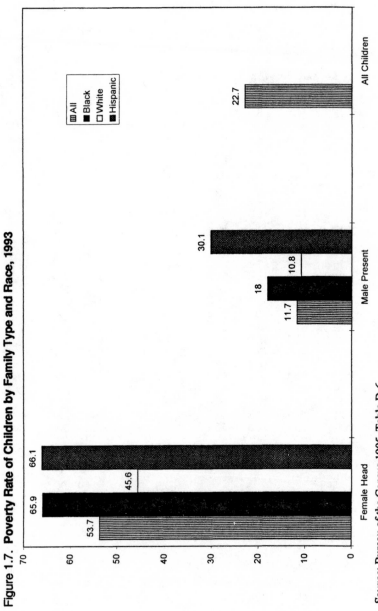

Figure 1.7. Poverty Rate of Children by Family Type and Race, 1993

Source: Bureau of the Census 1995, Table D-6.

developmentally (Korenman, Miller, and Sjaastad 1994). The National Commission on Children (press release, 1994) has found that children who grow up in mother-only families are at significantly greater risk of drug and alcohol addiction, mental illness, suicide, and criminality. More than two-thirds of incarcerated teenagers are fatherless boys. Additionally, children who experience poverty are more likely to suffer poverty as adults (Treiman and Hauser 1977; Solon 1992). These are the patterns and social pathologies that must be reversed if poverty in America is to be conquered.

Poverty Spells and the Limited Impact of Welfare

Most of the American poor are not poor for long periods of time. The average family that becomes poor will escape poverty within two years (Ruggles 1990; Gottschalk, McLanahan, and Sandefur 1994, 90). Escaping poverty, however, does not mean moving into the ranks of the middle-income. Most of the poor escape poverty by becoming the near-poor, and many of them will relapse into poverty. About 20 percent of all those who become poor remain poor for extended periods. Mother-only families are disproportionately represented in this group, and this is especially true when the mother is a member of a minority group. Bane and Ellwood (1986) found, for example, that "the average poor black child today appears to be in the midst of a poverty spell which will last for almost two decades." Thus, mother-only families, which constituted only about 37 percent of all the poor in 1993 (up from about 16% in 1960), are the largest long-term poverty group in American society and are the major consumers of welfare.

Only about half of all mother-only families receive welfare benefits. Those mother-only families who do receive benefits are the major nonaged welfare clients in America. Over 90 percent of all AFDC (Aid to Families with Dependent Children) recipients are members of mother-only families. Many of these families remain on AFDC for a decade or more. AFDC benefits are so low that they push only about 10 percent of recipient families over the poverty line (Danziger, Sandefur, and Weinberg 1994, 10). When food stamps and other noncash benefits are added to AFDC benefits, about one-third of mother-only families are removed from poverty. By contrast, over 80 percent of all elderly citizens receiving social welfare benefits escape poverty (Danziger, Sandefur, and Weinberg 1994, 9).

In summary, three reasons poverty has remained so high are: (1) mother-only families are becoming an increasingly large proportion of all American families; (2) mother-only families suffer very high rates of poverty; and (3) extant social policies and welfare programs do far too little to prevent or alleviate poverty among mother-only families.

The Organization of This Book

The following chapters attempt to dissect the problem of increasing poverty among women and their dependent children. The intent is to identify the most obvious causes and consequences of this growing poverty population; critique existing welfare, social, and private-sector programs; and evaluate policy alternatives and the new welfare approaches adopted in the last few years, including the reforms debated by Congress in 1995. Chapter 2 begins by providing an empirical analysis of the changes in the poverty population over the last two decades that have produced the feminization of poverty, with emphasis on female-headed families with children. It addresses the major questions about the feminization of poverty raised by researchers and provides an analysis of the impact of women's poverty on children.

Chapter 3 addresses the question of why women are increasingly the heads of families and spells out the major causes of poverty among women and their children. Chapter 4 critiques current welfare programs to delineate why they neither prevent poverty nor adequately meet the needs of poor women and their dependents. Chapter 5 reviews social welfare programs for women in major West European nations. The intent here is to provide insights into some innovative programs and experiments in other nations that might inform discussions of further reforms of American programs. Finally, chapter 6 critiques recent welfare reforms and discusses the program changes required to ameliorate the growing problem of poverty among women and their dependents.

Chapter 2

Poverty Trends and
the Feminization of Poverty

In recent years, America has fought a losing battle with poverty. This has not always been true. The post–World War II growth of the economy along with increasing government expenditures on social welfare programs reduced poverty by half between the late 1940s and the early 1960s. The same trends in both the economy and government expenditures cut poverty by another half by the early 1970s (Figure 2.1). Throughout the rest of the 1970s, both growth in average family incomes and the poverty rate stagnated. Two serious recessions between 1979 and 1983 drove down family incomes and significantly increased the poverty rate. Since 1983 average family incomes have continued to decline, earnings and income inequality have increased, and government expenditures for social welfare have decreased in real dollars, significantly increasing the overall poverty rate (Danziger and Weinberg 1994). The poverty rate in 1993 (15.1%) was the highest in a decade.

The exception to increasing rates of poverty has been the elderly. As Table 2.1 (p. 26) shows, in 1960 over a third of all Americans over sixty-five were poor. Significant increases in social welfare expenditures for the aged have reduced their poverty

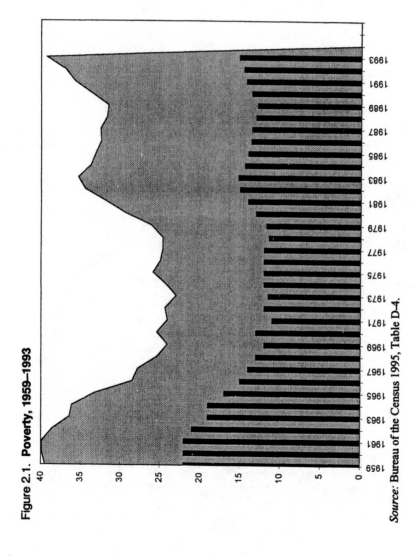

Figure 2.1. Poverty, 1959–1993

Millions of Poor

Percentage of Total Population

Source: Bureau of the Census 1995, Table D-4.

Table 2.1

Poverty Rate for Individuals in Selected Demographic Groups, 1959–1993

Year	Total poor	Elderly	Children[a]	Individuals in female-headed families[b]	Blacks	Hispanic origin[c]	Whites
1959	22.4	35.2	27.3	49.4	55.1	NA	18.1
1960	22.2	35.2	26.9	48.9	55.9	NA	17.8
1961	21.9	NA	25.6	48.1	NA	NA	17.4
1962	21.0	NA	25.0	50.3	NA	NA	16.4
1963	19.5	NA	23.1	47.7	NA	NA	15.3
1964	19.0	NA	23.0	44.4	NA	NA	14.9
1965	17.3	NA	21.0	46.0	NA	NA	13.3
1966	14.7	28.5	17.6	39.8	41.8	NA	11.3
1967	14.2	29.5	16.6	38.8	39.3	NA	11.0
1968	12.8	25.0	15.6	38.7	34.7	NA	10.0
1969	12.1	25.3	14.0	38.2	32.2	NA	9.5
1970	12.6	24.6	15.1	38.1	33.5	24.3	9.9
1971	12.5	21.6	15.3	38.7	32.5	NA	9.9
1972	11.9	18.6	15.1	38.2	33.3	22.8	9.0
1973	11.1	16.3	14.4	37.5	31.4	21.9	8.4
1974	11.2	14.6	15.4	36.5	30.3	23.0	8.6
1975	12.3	15.3	17.1	37.5	31.3	26.9	9.7
1976	11.8	15.0	16.0	37.3	31.1	24.7	9.1
1977	11.6	14.1	16.2	36.2	31.3	22.4	8.9
1978	11.4	14.0	15.9	35.6	30.6	21.6	8.7
1979	11.7	15.2	16.4	34.9	31.0	21.8	9.0
1980	13.0	15.7	18.3	36.7	32.5	25.7	10.2
1981	14.0	15.3	20.0	38.7	34.2	26.5	11.1
1982	15.0	14.6	21.9	40.6	35.6	29.9	12.0
1983	15.2	13.8	22.3	40.2	35.7	28.0	12.1
1984	14.4	12.4	21.5	38.4	33.8	28.4	11.5
1985	14.0	12.6	20.7	37.6	31.3	29.0	11.4
1986	13.6	12.4	20.5	38.3	31.1	27.3	11.0
1987	13.4	12.5	20.5	38.3	32.6	28.1	10.4
1988	13.0	12.0	19.5	37.2	31.3	26.7	10.1
1989	12.8	11.4	19.6	35.9	30.7	26.2	10.0
1990	13.5	12.2	20.6	37.2	31.9	28.1	10.7
1991	14.2	12.4	21.8	39.7	32.7	28.7	11.3
1992	14.5	12.9	21.9	38.5	33.3	29.3	11.6
1993	15.1	12.2	22.7	38.7	32.1	30.6	12.2

Source: Bureau of the Census (Various years [a]).

[a]All children including unrelated children.

[b]Does not include females living alone.

[c]Hispanic origin may be of any race; it is an overlapping category.

NA: Not available.

rate to about 12 percent, lower than the national average. Poverty among children, on the other hand, has been increasing. In 1993 children suffered their highest poverty rate (22.7%) since 1964. Poverty rates for Hispanics also increased, while rates for black Americans and female-headed households remain particularly high. In fact, the poverty rate for minorities, elderly widows, and children in mother-only families was as high in 1993 as it was in the 1950s (Table 2.1). In 1993, the vast majority of all the American poor were children (40%), the elderly (9.6%), members of female-headed families (37%), and unrelated individuals (21.4%) (Table 2.2 and Figures 2.2 and 2.3 [pp. 28–30]).

Progress against poverty has declined drastically since the 1970s for three major reasons. First, wages of less-skilled workers, compared to those of higher-skill workers, are declining. The gap between the incomes of college and non-college graduates, for example, is growing quite significantly. The declining demand for, and value of, less-skilled work is a very serious problem for millions of Americans. As Danziger and Weinberg point out: "If the incomes of all American families had grown at the same moderate rate as did the median, poverty in 1992 would have been somewhat below the 1973 rate" (1994, 19). This would have reduced the 1992 poverty population by about nine million people.

Second, adjusted for inflation, welfare spending has been declining. As we will detail in chapter 4, a family on assistance in the last decade received considerably less help in real dollars than did a similar family in the 1970s. Third, as noted in chapter 1, an increasing proportion of all American families are headed by single women, a family type that is particularly vulnerable to poverty. Below we will analyze in more depth the significant increase in the proportion of women and children among all the poor and the implications for American poverty and social welfare programs.

The Increase in Single Women and Children Among the Poor

The most significant change in the composition of the poor over the last three decades has been the dramatic increase in the pro-

Table 2.2

The Poverty Population, 1960–1993

	Percentage poor				Percentage of poor population			
	1960	1970	1980	1993	1960	1970	1980	1993
All Persons	22.2	12.6	13.0	15.1				
Race/ethnicity								
White	17.8	9.9	10.2	12.2	71.0	68.5	67.3	66.7
Black	55.9	33.5	32.5	33.1	29.0	30.0	29.3	27.7
Asian/Pacific Islander	NA	NA	17.2	15.3	NA	NA	2.4	2.9
Hispanic[a]	NA	24.3	25.7	30.6	NA	8.5	11.9	20.7
Family structure								
In families	20.7	10.9	11.5	13.6	87.6	80.0	77.2	76.2
Female household, no husband present	48.9	38.1	36.7	38.7	18.2	29.5	34.6	37.3
Unrelated individuals	45.2	32.9	22.9	22.1	12.4	20.0	21.3	21.4
Young and old								
Children under 18	26.5	14.9	17.9	22.0[b]	43.4	40.3	38.0	40.0
Adults 65 and older	35.2	24.5	15.7	12.2	14.1	18.5	13.2	9.6
Location								
Metropolitan areas	15.3	10.2	11.9	14.6	43.9	52.4	61.6	75.4
Central city	18.3	14.3	17.2	21.5	26.9	32.0	36.4	42.7
Suburbs	12.2	7.1	8.2	10.3	17.0	20.4	25.2	32.6
Outside metropolitan areas	33.2	17.0	15.4	17.2	56.1	47.6	38.4	24.6

Source: Bureau of the Census (Various years [a]).
[a]Hispanics may be of any race.
[b]Related children only.

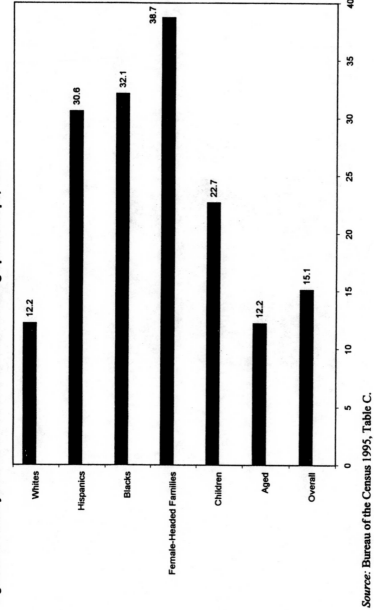

Figure 2.2. Poverty Rate for Individuals in Selected Demographic Groups, 1993

Source: Bureau of the Census 1995, Table C.

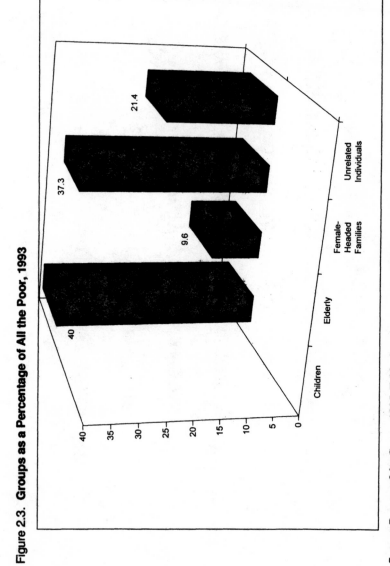

Figure 2.3. Groups as a Percentage of All the Poor, 1993

Source: Bureau of the Census 1995, Table C.

portion of all the poor who live in female-headed households. We will detail, by racial group, the dramatic increase in the proportion of women and children among all the poor. The data are then used to examine why this change has occurred. The analysis reveals that the key factor in explaining the rising proportion of women and children among all the poor is not an increasing rate of poverty for women and children or a decreasing rate of poverty for other family types.* Instead, it is simply the huge increase in the number of households headed by women.

Female-headed households suffer a high but rather steady rate of poverty. As the proportion of all such households has grown, their high rate of poverty has encompassed larger and larger numbers of poor women and children. Poverty, in other words, has become a matter not just of economics, but also of family structure.

The Increase in Mother-Only Families

In the early 1960s less than 10 percent of all families with children were headed by a single woman. Over the last twenty-five years the percentage has grown to almost one in four families with dependent children (Table 2.3, Figure 2.4 [p. 34]). All major racial groups have been affected by this trend, but it has been most dramatic among black families. By 1993 some 18 percent of all white families with children were headed by a single woman.

---

*An important caveat should be noted. The rate of poverty for all groups is determined by the Social Security Administration's calculation of the official poverty standard. This standard was first calculated in 1965 and backdated to 1959. Since 1969 the standard has been adjusted yearly according to changes in the Consumer Price Index. The yearly adjustments have been so low that the poverty standard has become an increasingly smaller proportion of median family income. For example, in 1959 the poverty standard for a family of four equaled 53 percent of median family income for a family of four. By 1993 the ratio for this family type had fallen to about 33 percent. Thus, the recent stability of the poverty rate for female-headed families in part reflects the failure of the poverty standard to maintain its historic relationship to median incomes.

Table 2.3

Mother-Only Families with Children Under 18, 1959–1993 (in thousands)

	Number	Percentage of all families with children	Number	Percentage of all white families with children	Number	Percentage of all black families with children	Number	Percentage of all Hispanic families with children
1993	8,758	24.0	5,361	18.3	3,084	55.8	1,167	28.1
1992	8,375	23.4	5,099	17.7	2,971	54.5	1,037	26.2
1991	7,991	22.9	4,967	17.5	2,771	53.9	972	26.8
1990	7,707	22.3	4,786	17.0	2,698	53.2	921	26.3
1989	7,445	21.7	4,627	16.5	2,624	52.1	848	25.6
1988	7,361	21.5	4,553	16.3	2,583	51.5	861	25.9
1987	7,216	21.2	4,548	16.3	2,453	50.3	865	27.0
1986	7,094	20.9	4,552	16.3	2,386	49.6	822	26.7
1985	6,892	20.5	4,470	16.1	2,269	48.9	771	25.9
1984	6,832	20.7	4,337	15.8	2,335	51.7	711	25.5
1983	6,622	20.2	4,210	15.4	2,244	50.0	660	24.5
1982	6,397	19.6	4,037	14.9	2,199	49.2	613	24.9
1981	6,488	19.9	4,237	15.6	2,118	47.5	622	25.6
1980	6,299	19.2	3,995	14.6	2,171	48.6	NA	NA

1979	6,035	18.6	3,866	14.1	2,063	48.0	502	22.7
1978	5,837	18.4	3,780	14.0	1,946	46.8	NA	NA
1977	5,709	18.0	3,735	13.9	1,878	45.7	NA	NA
1976	5,310	16.9	3,456	12.9	1,781	44.0	NA	NA
1975	5,119	16.3	3,406	12.6	1,651	42.6	NA	NA
1974	4,917	15.7	3,244	12.1	1,623	41.4	NA	NA
1973	4,597	14.8	2,988	11.2	1,538	40.1	NA	NA
1972	4,321	14.0	2,748	10.3	1,494	41.0	NA	NA
1971	4,077	13.3	2,664	10.0	1,369	37.4	NA	NA
1970	3,837	12.8	NA	NA	NA	NA	NA	NA
1969	3,384	11.3	NA	NA	NA	NA	NA	NA
1968	3,269	11.1	NA	NA	NA	NA	NA	NA
1967	3,190	11.0	NA	NA	NA	NA	NA	NA
1966	2,959	10.3	NA	NA	NA	NA	NA	NA
1965	2,873	10.2	NA	NA	NA	NA	NA	NA
1964	2,893	10.2	NA	NA	NA	NA	NA	NA
1963	2,833	10.0	NA	NA	NA	NA	NA	NA
1962	2,701	9.6	NA					
1961	2,687	9.7						
1960	2,619	9.7						
1959	2,544	9.4						

Source: Bureau of the Census 1995, Table D-6.
NA: Not available.

34

Figure 2.4. Mother-Only Families as a Percentage of All Families with Children, 1959–1993

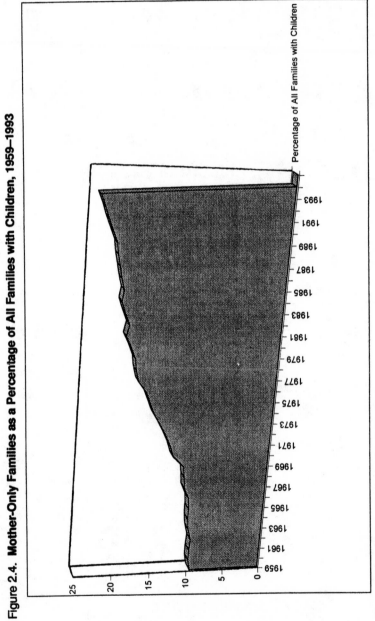

Source: Bureau of the Census 1995, Table D-6.

Among Hispanic families the rate reached 28.1 percent in 1993. By the late 1970s the rate for black families was almost 50 percent, a benchmark crossed by the early 1980s. In 1993 almost 56 percent of all black families with children were headed by a single woman. The economic consequences of these changes have been significant for each of these major groups.

Poor Mother-Only Families

The number of poor mother-only families increased from 1.5 million in 1959 to over 4 million in 1993 (Table 2.4). However, the rate of poverty for this family type did not significantly increase. In fact, the poverty rate for mother-only families was actually lower in 1993 than in 1959 (Table 2.4 [pp. 38–39). In 1959 almost 60 percent of all mother-only families were poor. In the last decade the poverty rate in these families has averaged about 45 percent. Still, the huge increase in mother-only families along with their high but rather steady rate of poverty has made this type of family the major poverty group in America. In the late 1950s and early 1960s, women headed less than 30 percent of all poor families with children. By the early 1970s over half of all poor families with children were headed by a woman, reaching some 60 percent by the late 1980s and into the early 1990s (Table 2.4 and Figure 2.5).

Table 2.4 shows how much more vulnerable mother-only families are than other family types. The poverty rate for all families with children, in fact, tracks the general trends in poverty over the last thirty years (see Figure 2.1 [p. 25]). The poverty rate declined during the 1970s, rose in the 1980s, and increased again in the early 1990s. Through these ups and downs, married-couple families demonstrated the strongest ability to cope economically. Their rate of poverty increased throughout the 1980s, but has remained below 10 percent, except in 1983, when it hit 10.1 percent. Over this same period, the number of families with children headed by a single male increased significantly from less than 100,000 in the mid-1970s to some 350,000 in 1993. The poverty rate for these male-headed families rose

Figure 2.5. Percentage of All Poor Families with Children, Headed by a Single Woman, 1959–1993

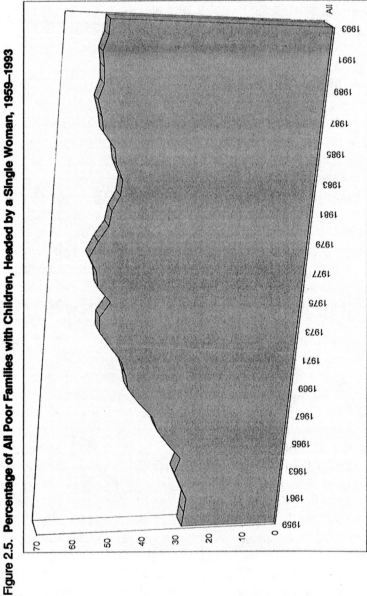

Source: Bureau of the Census 1995, Table D-6.

significantly, reaching some 22 percent in 1993. Still, this type of family composed only a little over 5 percent of all poor families with children in 1993.

Thus, the feminization of poverty is not the result of female-headed families' suffering increased economic problems over the years. This type of family has always been in severe economic jeopardy. The feminization of poverty has resulted not from increased vulnerability but from the huge increase in the number of these economically precarious families.

Table 2.5 (p. 40) shows that these trends are consistent across racial lines. The numbers of white, black, and Hispanic families with children headed by a single women have increased very significantly since the early 1960s, and at roughly the same rate of growth. Poor white and black mother-only families more than doubled between the early 1970s and 1993. The same trend is obvious for Hispanic families since the early 1980s, when data were first collected.

Black and Hispanic mother-only families suffer a rate of poverty that exceeds 50 percent, but the poverty rate for white mother-only families is also very high. In 1993 some 40 percent of all white mother-only families lived in poverty. Mother-only families, regardless of race, suffer extreme economic vulnerability, resulting in poverty in a majority of cases.

Poverty among other family types has also been increasing. As Table 2.4 shows, poverty among married-couple families, rather than declining, has increased from 6 percent in 1974 to 9 percent in 1993. This trend is consistent across racial lines. Between 1975 and 1993 the poverty rate for white married-couple families increased from 6.3 percent to 8.2 percent. There has been little change in the rate for black married-couple families. In 1973 14.5 percent of these families lived in poverty, and in 1993 the rate was 13.9 percent. Data are limited for Hispanics, but in 1987 the poverty rate for Hispanic married-couple families with children was 20.9 percent, and in 1993 it was 23.7 percent (Bureau of the Census 1995, D28).

A similar trend is found among the nation's small number of

Table 2.4

Poor Families with Children Under 18, 1959–1993 (in thousands)

	All families		Married-couple families		Male householder, no wife present		Female householder, no husband present		
	Number	Poverty rate	Number	Poverty rate	Number	Poverty rate	Number	Poverty rate	Percentage of all poor families with children
1993	6,751	18.5	2,363	9.0	354	22.5	4,034	46.1	59.7
1992	6,457	18.0	2,237	8.6	353	22.5	3,867	46.2	59.8
1991	6,170	17.7	2,106	8.3	297	19.6	3,767	47.1	61.0
1990	5,676	16.4	1,990	7.8	260	18.8	3,426	44.5	60.3
1989	5,308	15.5	1,872	7.3	246	18.1	3,190	42.8	60.0
1988	5,373	15.7	1,847	7.2	232	18.0	3,294	44.7	61.3
1987	5,465	16.1	1,963	7.7	221	16.8	3,281	45.5	60.0
1986	5,516	16.3	2,050	8.0	202	17.8	3,264	46.0	59.2
1985	5,586	16.7	2,258	8.9	197	17.1	3,131	45.4	56.0
1984	5,662	17.2	2,344	9.4	194	18.1	3,124	45.7	55.2
1983	5,871	17.9	2,557	10.1	192	20.2	3,122	47.1	53.2
1982	5,712	17.5	2,470	9.8	184	20.6	3,059	47.8	53.5
1981	5,191	15.9	2,199	8.7	115	14.0	2,877	44.3	55.4

Year									
1979	4,081	12.6	1,573	6.1	116	15.5	2,392	39.6	58.6
1978	4,060	12.8	1,495	5.9	103	14.7	2,462	42.2	60.6
1977	4,081	12.9	1,602	6.3	95	14.8	2,384	41.8	58.4
1976	4,060	12.9	1,623	6.4	94	15.4	2,343	44.1	57.7
1975	4,172	13.3	1,855	7.2	65	11.7	2,252	44.0	54.0
1974	3,789	12.1	1,558	6.0	84	15.4	2,147	43.7	56.6
1973	3,520	11.4	NA	NA	NA	NA	1,987	43.2	56.4
1972	3,621	11.8	NA	NA	NA	NA	1,925	44.5	53.2
1971	3,683	12.0	NA	NA	NA	NA	1,830	44.9	49.7
1970	3,491	11.6	NA	NA	NA	NA	1,680	43.8	48.1
1969	3,226	10.8	NA	NA	NA	NA	1,519	44.9	47.1
1968	3,347	11.4	NA	NA	NA	NA	1,459	44.6	43.6
1967	3,586	12.4	NA	NA	NA	NA	1,418	44.5	39.5
1966	3,734	13.4	NA	NA	NA	NA	1,410	47.1	37.7
1965	4,379	15.6	NA	NA	NA	NA	1,499	52.2	34.2
1964	4,771	16.9	NA	NA	NA	NA	1,439	49.7	30.2
1963	4,991	17.6	NA	NA	NA	NA	1,578	55.7	31.6
1962	5,460	19.4	NA	NA	NA	NA	1,613	59.7	29.5
1961	5,500	19.9	NA	NA	NA	NA	1,505	56.0	27.4
1960	5,328	19.7	NA	NA	NA	NA	1,476	56.3	27.7
1959	5,443	20.3	NA	NA	NA	NA	1,525	59.9	28.0

Source: Bureau of the Census 1995, Table D-6.
NA: Not available.

Table 2.5

Poor Mother-Only Families with Children Under 18 by Race, 1959–1993
(in thousands)

Year	White		Black		Hispanic	
	Number	Poverty rate	Number	Poverty rate	Number	Poverty rate
1993	2,123	39.6	1,780	57.7	706	60.5
1992	2,021	39.6	1,706	57.4	598	57.7
1991	1,969	39.6	1,676	60.5	584	60.1
1990	1,814	37.9	1,513	56.1	536	58.2
1989	1,671	36.1	1,415	53.9	491	57.9
1988	1,740	38.2	1,452	56.2	510	59.2
1987	1,742	38.3	1,437	58.6	527	60.9
1986	1,812	39.8	1,384	58.0	489	59.5
1985	1,730	38.7	1,336	58.9	493	64.0
1984	1,682	38.8	1,364	58.4	447	62.8
1983	1,676	39.8	1,362	60.7	418	63.4
1982	1,584	39.3	1,401	63.7	391	63.8
1981	1,564	36.9	1,261	59.5	374	60.0
1980	1,433	35.9	1,217	56.0	NA	NA
1979	1,211	31.3	1,129	54.7	288	57.3
1978	1,268	33.5	1,144	58.4	NA	NA
1977	1,261	33.8	1,081	57.5	NA	NA
1976	1,260	36.4	1,043	58.6	NA	NA
1975	1,272	37.3	949	58.5	NA	NA
1974	1,180	36.4	949	58.5	NA	NA
1973	1,053	35.2	905	58.8	NA	NA
1972	970	35.3	912	61.0	NA	NA
1971	982	36.9	821	60.0	NA	NA
1970	NA	NA	NA	NA	NA	NA
1969	NA	NA	NA	NA	NA	NA
1968	792	36.0	NA	NA	NA	NA
1967	748	34.9	NA	NA	NA	NA
1966	803	38.4	NA	NA	NA	NA
1965	867	43.2	NA	NA	NA	NA
1964	814	40.3	NA	NA	NA	NA
1963	882	45.0	NA	NA	NA	NA
1962	908	49.2	NA	NA	NA	NA
1961	892	46.4	NA	NA	NA	NA
1960	905	47.1	NA	NA	NA	NA
1959	948	51.7	NA	NA	NA	NA

Source: Bureau of the Census 1995, Table D-6.
NA: Not available.

father-only families, including those below the poverty level. As noted above, the rate of poverty for father-only families increased between 1974 and 1993. This was also true for each major racial group. The poverty rate for white father-only families increased from 11 percent in 1975 to 19.5 percent in 1993. The overall rate is higher for black father-only families, increasing from 26.2 percent in 1974 to 31.6 percent in 1993. Among Hispanics the data are limited but show an increase from 25.2 percent in 1987 to 27.6 percent in 1993 (Table 2.6).

Women and children, then, are not a majority of the poor because the poverty rate has risen for this type of family while falling for other types. They are a majority because this type of family, which suffers a very high rate of poverty, has been growing faster than any other type of family in America.

The Increase in Child Poverty

Poverty among children has risen particularly rapidly since the early 1970s. By the 1980s there were more poor children (an average of 12.5 million) than in any period since the early to mid-1960s (Figure 2.6 [p. 43]). The number of poor children increased by over 3 million in the short period between 1979 and 1984 (Table 1.4). This was true despite a decrease of 9 million in the total population of children between 1968 and 1983. By the 1980s the poverty rate for children averaged over 20 percent. This was the highest rate of poverty among children since the early 1960s. In 1993 there were 15.7 million poor children, 22.7 percent of all American children.

Figure 2.7 [p. 44] shows the statistical relationship between the growth of mother-only families and the increasing rate of poverty for children. The relationship is quite strong, suggesting a causal relationship between the growth of mother-only families and the expanding rate of poverty among American children. As a larger proportion of all American families with children are headed by single women, poverty among children can be expected to worsen.

Table 2.6

Poor Father-Only Families with Children Under 18 by Race, 1959–1993
(in thousands)

	White		Black		Hispanic	
Year	Number	Poverty rate	Number	Poverty rate	Number	Poverty rate
1993	235	19.5	93	31.6	66	27.6
1992	246	19.7	83	33.5	89	38.2
1991	196	16.5	77	31.7	60	29.4
1990	167	16.0	73	27.3	48	28.1
1989	162	15.0	77	33.8	42	26.8
1988	147	14.5	78	31.7	33	26.4
1987	153	14.6	61	27.5	35	25.2
1986	132	14.5	58	31.5	NA	NA
1985	138	14.9	53	29.0	NA	NA
1984	117	13.6	62	35.5	NA	NA
1983	123	16.8	58	31.1	NA	NA
1982	120	17.4	58	32.7	NA	NA
1981	75	11.6	34	25.0	NA	NA
1980	100	16.0	34	24.0	NA	NA
1979	82	14.1	26	18.4	NA	NA
1978	60	11.4	40	25.5	NA	NA
1977	55	11.3	30	21.3	NA	NA
1976	64	13.2	28	23.3	NA	NA
1975	48	11.0	16	14.8	NA	NA
1974	NA	NA	27	26.2	NA	NA
1973	NA	NA	NA	NA	NA	NA
1972	NA	NA	NA	NA	NA	NA
1971	NA	NA	NA	NA	NA	NA
1970	NA	NA	NA	NA	NA	NA
1969	NA	NA	NA	NA	NA	NA
1968	NA	NA	NA	NA	NA	NA
1967	NA	NA	NA	NA	NA	NA
1966	NA	NA	NA	NA	NA	NA
1965	NA	NA	NA	NA	NA	NA
1964	NA	NA	NA	NA	NA	NA
1963	NA	NA	NA	NA	NA	NA
1962	NA	NA	NA	NA	NA	NA
1961	NA	NA	NA	NA	NA	NA
1960	NA	NA	NA	NA	NA	NA
1959	NA	NA	NA	NA	NA	NA

Source: Bureau of the Census 1995, Table D-6.
NA: Not available.

43

Figure 2.6. Poverty Rate of Children, 1959–1993

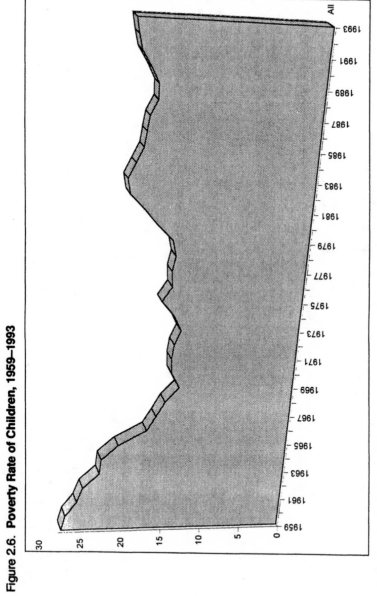

Source: Bureau of the Census (Various years [a]).

Figure 2.7. Relationship Between the Growth of Mother-Only Families and Children's Poverty

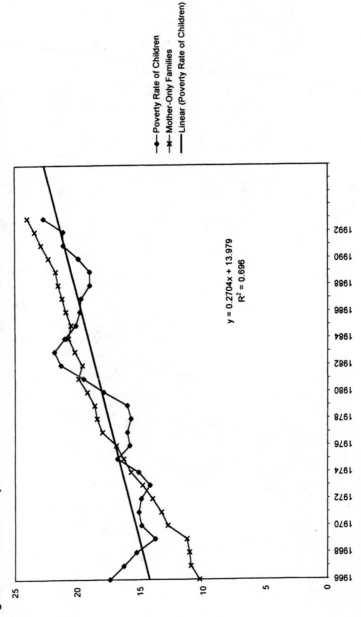

y = 0.2704x + 13.979
R^2 = 0.696

●— Poverty Rate of Children
✳— Mother-Only Families
—— Linear (Poverty Rate of Children)

Source: Calculations by the author.

Analyzing child poverty by race also yields some interesting insights. As Table 1.3 and Figure 1.5 show, the majority of all poor children are white. In 1993, 62 percent of all poor children were white, about the same percentage as during the 1960s and 1970s. The poverty rate for white children has averaged 16 percent since 1987, reaching 17.8 percent in 1993. This is the highest rate of poverty for white children since the early 1960s and a significant increase over the rate in the 1970s, which averaged 11 percent.

Poverty among black children has also increased since the early 1970s. In 1993 there were 5.1 million poor black children. This was an increase of about 1 million children just since 1986. The poverty rate for black children is truly staggering. It is more than two and a half times the much-too-high rate for white children. The rate of poverty for black children averaged 41 percent in the 1970s, rose modestly in the 1980s, and exceeded 46 percent in the early 1990s (see Table 1.3).

Data on Hispanic children have been available only for some twenty years, but they show that poverty among children in these families is also very high and increasing. The poverty rate for Hispanic children expanded from 30.2 percent in 1976 to 40.9 percent in 1993.

Poor Children in Mother-Only Families

The poverty rate for children in mother-only families is particularly severe across racial lines (see Tables 1.4, 1.5, and 2.7 and Figures 1.7 and 2.8 [p. 47]). As Table 2.7 shows, the percentage of all poor children that are in mother-only families more than doubled between 1959 and 1993, increasing from some 24 percent of all poor children to 54 percent in 1993. The overall poverty rate for these children declined during the 1960s, but remained over 50 percent through 1993 (Figure 1.6).

Poor White Children

The number of poor white children in mother-only families increased from 2.4 million in 1959 to 4.1 million in 1993. In 1993,

Table 2.7

Poor Children in Mother-Only Families by Race, 1959, 1970, 1980, 1993 (in thousands)

	Number	Percentage of all poor children	Poverty rate	White poor children	Percentage of all white poor children	Poverty rate	Black poor children	Percentage of all black poor children	Poverty rate	Hispanic poor children	Percentage of all Hispanic poor children	Poverty rate
1993	8,503	54.0	53.7	4,102	45.0	45.6	4,104	81.6	65.9	1,673	45.6	66.1
1980	5,866	52.8	50.8	2,813	41.3	41.6	2,944	75.4	64.8	809	47.1	65.0
1970	4,689	45.8	53.0	2,247	36.6	43.1	2,383	60.7	67.7	NA	NA	NA
1959	4,145	24.1	72.2	2,420	21.2	64.6	1,475	29.4	81.6	NA	NA	NA

Source: Bureau of the Census 1995.

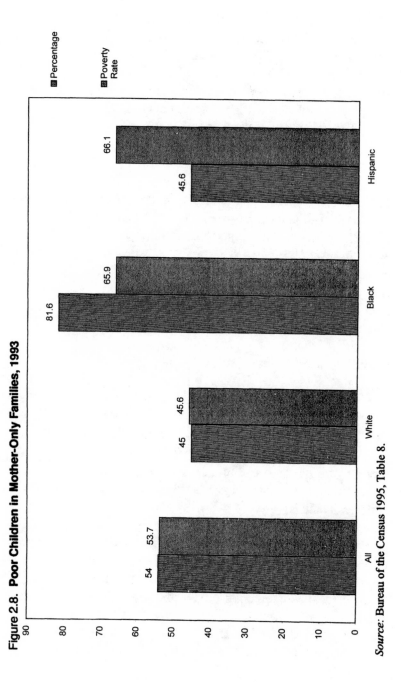

Figure 2.8. Poor Children in Mother-Only Families, 1993

Source: Bureau of the Census 1995, Table 8.

45 percent of all poor white children lived in a family headed by a single woman. This represents a very substantial increase since 1959, when only 21.2 percent lived in mother-only families. The poverty rate for white children declined in the 1960s and early 1970s but has remained in the high- to mid-40-percent range since the early 1980s. In 1993, 45.6 percent of all white children in mother-only families were poor.

Poor Black Children

The number of poor black children in mother-only families increased by 180 percent between 1959 and 1993. The 1.5 million poor black children in mother-only families in 1959 increased to 4.1 million in 1993. In 1959 slightly less than 30 percent of all poor black children lived in a female-headed family. In 1993 almost 82 percent of all poor black children lived with a single mother. Almost two-thirds of all black children in these families live in poverty.

Poor Hispanic Children

The number of poor Hispanic children in mother-only families almost tripled between 1974 and 1993, increasing from 600,000 to 1.7 million (Table 2.7). During this period almost half of all poor Hispanic children lived in mother-only families. The poverty rate for children in these families is similar to the rate for black children in mother-only families: about two-thirds of the children live in poverty.

In mother-only families, children suffer the highest rates of poverty when the mother has never married and when the mother is married but the spouse is absent (Table 2.8 and Figure 2.9 [p. 50]). Children in mother-only families that resulted from divorce or death of the spouse have the lowest rates of poverty, although even in these families the poverty rate is very high. Not only are poverty rates higher in families in which the mother has never married, but these families tend to be poor and on welfare

Table 2.8

Living Arrangements of Children in Mother-Only Families, 1993

	Total	Marital status of mother			
		Divorced	Married—spouse absent	Widowed	Never married
Total number of children	15,586	5,687	3,739	649	5,511
Percentage below poverty level		(36.5) 38.4	(24.0) 58.9	(4.2) 32.3	(35.3) 66.3
White	9,256	4,441	2,322	478	2,015
Percentage below poverty level		(48.0) 34.6	(25.0) 54.6	(5.2) 28.6	(21.8) 61.1
Black	5,757	1.032	1,272	137	3,317
Percentage below poverty level		(17.9) 53.4	(22.1) 67.8	(2.4) 45.8	(57.6) 69.8
Hispanic	2,176	579	649	101	848
Percentage below poverty level		(26.6) 48.3	(29.8) 68.7	(4.6) 48.9	(39.0) 72.7

Source: Bureau of the Census 1994b, Table 6.
Note: Figures in parentheses are percentages of total poor children in each category.

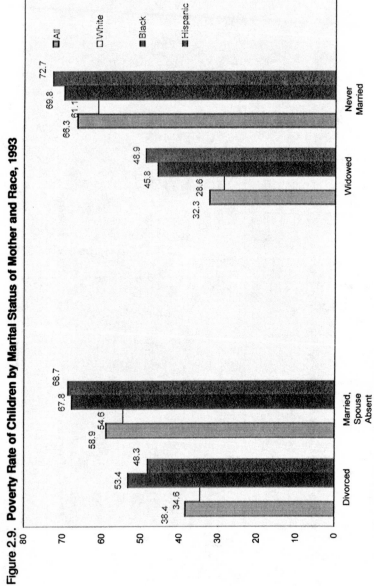

Figure 2.9. Poverty Rate of Children by Marital Status of Mother and Race, 1993

Source: Bureau of the Census 1994b, Table 6.

for longer periods than other mother-only families. Thus, children in these families tend to be in jeopardy for particularly long periods.

Conclusions

The data presented show the changes in poverty demographics that have resulted in women and their dependent children becoming an increasingly large proportion of all the official poor in America. At present over half of all the poor children in America live in homes headed by single women, including over 80 percent of all poor black children.

The rate of poverty for female-headed households has always been high, and it has not changed dramatically over the last fifteen years (see the caveat in the footnote, page 31). What has changed is the number of female-headed households. As this type of household has increased, the high rate of poverty experienced by this type of family unit has greatly increased the number of poor women and children.

A review of American welfare programs in chapter 4 will show that American welfare programs have become increasingly less effective in ameliorating poverty, in part because they have not been revised to reflect the changing demographics of American families or the changing composition of the poverty population. Chapter 6 will examine the welfare reforms of 1995 in terms of how responsive they are to these very important changes. But first, chapter 3 addresses the question of why such an increasingly large proportion of all families are headed by single women and why these families suffer such high rates of poverty.

Mother-Only Families:
Growth and Causes of Poverty

This chapter first seeks to explain why an increasingly large proportion of American families with children are headed by single women. Second, it provides insight into why mother-only families suffer such high rates of poverty. Understanding both topics is critical to designing policies to remediate poverty among women and their children.

As noted in chapter 1, there are two major reasons the number of mother-only families has increased so dramatically. The first is greatly increased rates of divorce and separation. The second is significantly higher rates of out-of-wedlock births. Table 2.8 shows that divorce and separation was the reason for 60 percent of all mother-only families in 1993, with another 35.3 percent the result of out-of-wedlock births. Only about 4 percent of all mother-only families result from women being widowed.

Between 1970 and 1993 out-of-wedlock births became an increasingly significant cause of mother-only families, especially among black families. In 1970 only about 7 percent of all mother-only families were the result of out-of-wedlock births. This included a little over 3 percent of white families and about 16 percent of black mother-only families (Table 3.1). By 1993, 35.3 percent of all children, including 21.8 percent of all white, 57.6 percent of all black, and 39 percent of all Hispanic children, lived with a mother who had never married (Table 2.8).

The data in Table 3.2 (p. 55) show two additional points of importance. First, close to half of all the poor people in mother-only families are in families where the mother has never been married (45% in 1992). Second, the rate of poverty in families where the mother has never married is higher than the rate for intact families or mother-only families that result from divorce or death of the spouse. In 1993 the median income for two-parent families was $43,578, while it was $17,014 for divorced mothers and only $9,272 for never-married mothers. One reason for the differential in income is that about half of all never-married mothers do not have a high school education. Given the education and income differences, it is not surprising that while about 11 percent of all children in two-parent families in 1993 were poor, the poverty rate for children living with a divorced or never-married mother was considerably higher: 38 percent and 66 percent respectively.

Divorce and Separation

One reason for the growth in out-of-wedlock births is that increasingly women of childbearing age are single. Women are entering their first marriage later and divorcing more frequently. In 1950 the average age of first marriage was 20.3; in 1985 it was 23.3; and by 1993 it was 24.5 (Bureau of the Census 1994b, vii; Bureau of the Census 1994a, Table 142). In 1950 only about one-fourth of all twenty- to twenty-four-year-old women had never been married. By 1993 the proportion had risen to 66.8 percent (Bureau of the Census 1994b, ix; U.S. House 1994, 1109).

Divorce and separation have increased dramatically over the same period (Bane 1976; Cherlin 1981; Clayton and Voss 1977; Glick and Spanier 1980; Moore and Waite 1981). Figure 3.1 [p. 56] shows the marital status of all Americans over eighteen in 1970 and 1993. In 1970 some 4.3 million adults (3.2%) were divorced. By

Table 3.1

Families with Children Present by Race, Selected Years

Subject	All races					White			Black		
	1970	1980	1985	1988	1992	1970	1988	1992	1970	1988	1992
				Thousands of families							
Total with children under 18	29,631	32,151	33,352	34,344	35,379	26,115	28,102	28,847	3,219	5,057	5,164
Two-parent family groups	25,823	25,231	24,573	24,977	24,880	23,477	22,012	21,909	2,071	2,055	1,948
One-parent family groups	3,808	6,920	8,779	9,367	10,499	2,638	6,090	6,938	1,148	3,002	3,216
Maintained by mother	3,415	6,230	7,737	8,146	9,028	2,330	5,110	5,753	1,063	2,812	2,994
Never married	248	1,063	2,208	2,707	3,284	73	1,050	1,391	173	1,605	1,799
Spouse absent	1,377	1,743	1,732	1,776	1,947	796	1,127	1,341	570	585	548
Separated	962	1,483	1,524	1,499	1,658	477	941	1,146	479	515	482
Divorced	1,109	2,721	3,228	3,121	3,349	930	2,568	2,692	172	471	550
Widowed	682	703	569	544	448	531	356	328	148	149	97
Maintained by father	393	692	1,042	1,221	1,472	307	989	1,186	85	191	222
				Percent distribution							
Total with children under 18	100.0	100.0	100.0	100.0	100.0	100.0	100.0	100.0	100.0	100.0	100.0
Two-parent family groups	87.1	78.5	73.6	72.7	70.3	89.9	78.3	75.9	64.3	40.6	37.7
One-parent family groups	12.9	21.5	26.3	27.3	29.7	10.1	21.7	24.1	35.7	59.4	62.3
Maintained by mother	11.5	19.4	23.2	23.7	25.5	8.9	18.1	19.9	33.0	55.6	58.0
Never married	.8	3.3	6.6	7.9	9.3	.3	3.7	4.8	5.4	31.7	34.8
Spouse absent	4.6	5.4	5.2	5.2	5.5	3.0	4.0	4.6	17.7	11.6	10.6
Separated	3.2	4.6	4.6	4.4	4.7	1.8	3.3	4.0	14.9	10.2	9.3
Divorced	3.7	8.5	9.7	9.1	9.5	3.6	9.1	9.3	5.3	9.3	10.7
Widowed	2.3	2.2	1.7	1.6	1.3	2.0	1.3	1.1	4.6	2.9	1.9
Maintained by father	1.3	2.2	3.1	3.6	4.2	1.2	3.5	4.1	2.6	3.8	4.3

Source: Bureau of the Census (Various years [b]).

Note: Family groups consist of family households, related subfamilies, and unrelated subfamilies. Numbers may not sum to totals due to rounding.

Table 3.2

Persons Living in Mother-Only Families by Mother's Marital Status, Family Living Arrangement, and Family Poverty Status, 1992
(in thousands)

Family type defined by mother's marital status	Total	Family living arrangement			
		Independent families	Extended families	Cohabitating	Unrelated families
Total number of persons	26,609	18,455	4,379	2,240	1,535
Never married	9,351	5,555	2,465	910	420
Separated/other	6,097	4,725	815	262	296
Divorced	9,912	7,226	945	1,006	734
Widowed	1,248	948	155	61	84
Total number of poor persons	13,001	9,524	1,463	1,281	733
Never married	5,806	3,963	936	639	269
Separated/other	3,357	2,744	302	141	170
Divorced	3,472	2,554	182	475	261
Widowed	365	263	43	26	32
Total poverty rate (percent poor)	48.9	51.6	33.4	57.2	47.7
Never married	62.1	71.3	38.0	70.2	63.9
Separated/other	55.1	58.1	37.1	53.9	57.6
Divorced	35.0	35.3	19.2	47.2	35.6
Widowed	29.3	27.8	28.0	NA	38.4
Total number of families	9,339	6,134	1,799	865	541
Never married	3,448	1,879	1,063	354	152
Separated/other	1,974	1,465	303	102	104
Divorced	3,497	2,483	373	386	256
Widowed	420	308	60	23	29

Source: Table prepared by Congressional Research Service (CRS), based on analysis of the March 1993 *Current Population Survey* (CPS) microdata files.

1993 the number had risen to 16.6 million, 8.9 percent of all adults. Black women have the highest rate of divorce, Hispanic women the lowest.

Divorce, then, has played a major role in altering family relationships. The early 1970s were the first years in American history when more marriages ended in divorce than in death.

56

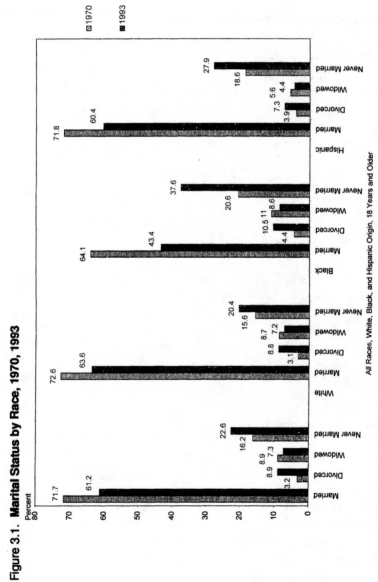

Figure 3.1. Marital Status by Race, 1970, 1993

Percent

All Races, White, Black, and Hispanic Origin, 18 Years and Older

Source: Bureau of the Census 1994, p. vi.

Cherlin (1981, 23) estimates that almost one-half of the marriages that have taken place since the early 1970s will end in divorce. When divorce occurs, remarriage is now less likely. The remarriage rate for women age twenty-five to forty-four declined by over one-third between 1970 and 1993.

Out-of-Wedlock Births

Births to unwed mothers is the fastest-growing cause of mother-only families. Since 1950 such births have increased more than eightfold, rising from 142,000 in 1950 to 1.2 million in 1991. In 1991 almost 30 percent of all children born in America had an unwed mother. Numerically there are considerably more white than black children born out of wedlock each year, but the rate of illegitimacy is two and a half times higher in the black population (Table 3.3).

In 1993, 22 percent of all white children and 68 percent of all black children were born to unwed mothers. In 1993 there were 6.3 million children (27% of all children) living with a single parent who had never married. As recently as 1983 there were 3.7 million such children, and in 1960 only 243,000.

Why Have Divorce and Unwed Births Increased?

The huge increases in rates of divorce and births to unmarried women constitute two of the most important demographic changes in American families in the twentieth century. The changes significantly alter life patterns such as sexual roles, parenting, careers, and social interactions. The changes have massive implications for social policy. So why have they occurred? Below we examine the four major reasons most often offered as explanations.

Male Employment and Earnings

Wilson and Neckerman (1986) and other scholars have argued that marital instability and the epidemic of out-of-wedlock births are in

Table 3.3

Number and Rate of Births to Unmarried Women by Race and Age of Mother, 1980 and 1991

Age	Out-of-wedlock births			Rate per 1,000 unmarried women		
	Total	White	Black	Total	White	Black
1980						
Under 15	9,024	3,144	5,707	NA	NA	NA
15 to 19	262,777	127,984	128,022	27.6	16.2	89.2
20 to 24	237,265	112,854	117,423	40.9	24.4	115.1
25 to 29	99,583	46,872	49,077	34.0	20.7	83.9
30 to 34	40,984	20,565	18,766	21.1	13.6	48.2
35 to 39	13,187	7,073	5,513	9.7	6.8	19.6
40 and over	2,927	1,571	1,229	2.6	1.8	5.6
Total (ages 15–44)	665,747	320,063	325,737	29.4	17.6	82.9
1991						
Under 15	10,968	4,346	6,298	NA	NA	NA
15 to 19	357,483	207,035	139,325	44.8	32.8	108.5
20 to 24	429,094	251,228	163,532	68.0	51.5	147.5
25 to 29	234,593	136,727	89,198	56.5	44.6	100.9
30 to 24	123,901	72,484	46,370	38.1	31.1	60.1
35 to 39	48,353	29,607	16,357	18.0	15.2	25.6
40 and over	9,377	6,075	2,670	3.8	3.2	5.4
Total (ages 15–44)	1,213,769	707,502	463,750	45.2	34.6	89.5

Source: National Center for Health Statistics 1993. Data are for 1993 and 1980.
Note: Race is determined by race of the child for 1980 and by race of the mother for 1991.
NA: Not available.

part the result of decreasing job opportunities for males, especially inner-city minorities with low skills. Wilson and Neckerman's argument is that when young men cannot earn enough to support a family, they avoid the responsibility of marriage, or may be rejected by women as suitable mates. There is some evidence to support their argument. In a recent poll, 77 percent of young women said that a well-paying job was an essential requirement for a husband (Casey Foundation 1995, 5). There is also a high correlation between male income levels and their rate of marriage. Among men in their thirties, those earning $50,000 a year or more are almost twice as likely to be married as those earning less than $10,000 (Casey Foundation 1995, 5). Earnings levels for young men, especially those poorly educated and minority, are also declining. Between 1972 and 1992 the median earned income of men aged twenty-five to thirty-four, in inflation-adjusted dollars, fell by 26 percent. In 1993 about half of all black and Hispanic men between the ages of twenty-five and thirty-four did not earn enough to support a family of four above the poverty level (Casey Foundation 1995, 6, 7).

Despite declines in real-dollar income for young men, the evidence suggests that the problem is not an actual shortage of jobs (Jencks 1992, 127; Blank 1994, 171). Over the last three decades growth in jobs has exceeded population growth. The problem is a shortage of jobs that pay low-skill workers well and of entry-level jobs that lead to middle-income employment. This is true regardless of whether those jobs are in service or manufacturing. In America's increasingly international and technologically sophisticated economy, there are decreasing economic opportunities for low-skill workers, regardless of race (Gottschalk and Moffitt 1994; Cutler and Katz 1992). The result is that those workers with a high school education or less entering the job market today can expect to enjoy lower incomes than did their fathers (Blank 1994). The opposite is true for college graduates, who can expect to earn incomes equivalent or superior to their fathers'.

Unemployment rates for teenage and minority males are very high. In 1993, for example, the unemployment rate for all males was 7.1 percent. However, for black and Hispanic males the rate was 13.8 and 10.4 percent, respectively. For white males the rate was 6.2 percent. Black unemployment has been above 10 percent and approximately double the white rate since the mid-1970s. The unemployment rate for black males twenty to twenty-four years old has averaged about 20 percent since 1980

(Bureau of the Census 1994a, Table 628). For teenage males the unemployment rate remains quite high. In 1993 the unemployment rate for teenagers (16–19) was 17.6 percent for whites, 40.2 percent for blacks, and 26.2 percent for Hispanics (Bureau of the Census 1994a, Table 628).

The combination of declining wages and high rates of unemployment has played a role in lowering the labor force participation rate of all low-income or poorly educated males over the last two decades (Bureau of the Census 1994a, Table 617). In recent years only about 75 percent of all males with less than a high school education have reported any type of employment. This contrasts with a labor force participation rate of over 90 percent for men with four or more years of college, regardless of race. The decline in work participation has been even more substantial for low-income black males. In recent years only about 55 percent have reported any employment (Juhn 1992). Some research suggests that especially among black males, unreported or off-the-books employment might explain some of the decline in official employment rates (Juhn 1992).

The evidence, then, does support the argument that declining wages, high unemployment, and decreasing rates of employment characterize a larger percentage of all males today than in the past (Bound and Holzer 1993; Bound and Freeman 1992; Bound and Johnson 1992). The question is: What is the impact of these changes on family structure? The evidence is mixed. Wilson and Neckerman (1986) compared the ratio of employed black men to employed black women in the same age cohort and found a significant decline since the 1970s. This decrease in employed black men occurred at the same time that marriage rates of blacks were declining quite dramatically. However, Mare and Winship (1991) found that only about 20 percent of the decrease in marriage rates for black men can be explained by their lower rates of employment. Testa (1991), Ellwood and Crane (1990), and Ellwood and Rodda (1991) also found that changes in employment patterns of males, white and black, are rather modest compared to the very substantial declines in rates of marriage. Thus, while male earnings, and rates of employment and unemployment, are related to marriage and perhaps divorce, this is just one factor contributing to the major increase in mother-only families (Lichter, McLaughlin, Kephart, and Landry 1992; Mare and Winship 1991).

Female Employment

A second reason often put forth for increased rates of divorce and births to unmarried women is the independence women increasingly enjoy because of their careers. Over the last thirty years women have greatly increased their percentage of all college graduates and their role in the job market (Dechter and Smock 1994). A slightly larger proportion of single women than married women are employed, but, over the last twenty years particularly, more married women have balanced career and family roles. Low-income single women have not significantly increased their employment rates over the same period, but, unlike low-income males, their level of employment has not declined. In 1993, women constituted about 46 percent of the total labor force, up from 36 percent in 1970 (Bureau of the Census 1994a, Table 615). Over 66 percent of single women and 59 percent of all married women were employed (Bureau of the Census 1994a, Table 625).

The evidence indicates that when women have employment or other independent sources of income, they are somewhat more inclined to leave bad marriages, take longer to remarry, and are more willing to have children outside of marriage (Groeneveld, Hannan, and Tuma 1983; Garfinkel and McLanahan 1986; Ellwood and Bane 1985; Bassi 1987; Garfinkel and McLanahan 1994, 211). The impact of employment is modest but often important (see Cain 1987; Bane and Ellwood 1994, 109–113).

Changing Social Mores

The great social movements of the 1960s have been credited with liberalizing public attitudes toward single parenthood and divorce (Magnet 1993). Certainly the stigma associated with either behavior has declined significantly over the last thirty years (Garfinkel and McLanahan 1986, 82), and behavior such as premarital sex is both more common and more accepted (Bane and Ellwood 1994, 114). It is reasonable to assume that a more accepting public attitude has made it easier for adults to make these choices. As we will detail in later chapters, however, the huge increase in out-of-wedlock births seems to be creating a backlash that is reflected in many of the more recent welfare reform proposals.

The Availability of Welfare

While the public tends to believe that the availability of welfare has had a major impact on divorce, remarriage, and out-of-wedlock births, the best evidence suggests that the effect may be modest. Danziger et al. (1982), Ellwood and Bane (1985), and Bassi (1987) all found a significant link between welfare receipt and divorce. Garfinkel and McLanahan (1986) concluded that while welfare receipt delayed remarriage, the implications for divorce and out-of-wedlock births are more limited. Garfinkel and McLanahan (1986) reported that the increase in welfare benefits between 1960 and 1975 contributed to about 15 percent of the growth in mother-only families, rising to about 30 percent of the increase among the low-income population (Garfinkel and McLanahan 1994, 211). Moffitt's review of the empirical research reached approximately the same conclusions (Moffitt 1992).

Acs (1993), in a very comprehensive evaluation, found little relationship between state AFDC benefits and state birth rates. Acs's findings are consistent with the major body of research on this topic (Ellwood and Bane 1985; Duncan and Hoffman 1988; Plotnick 1989). The out-of-wedlock birth rate, in other words, is not higher in states that pay high AFDC benefits than the rate in states that pay very low benefits. In fact, Mississippi, one of the lowest-paying states in the nation, has one of the highest out-of-wedlock birth rates. Some critics have argued that the amount of the state grant is less important than the fact that an out-of-wedlock birth results in some level of cash benefit. The only way to test this argument would be to cut off additional payments to mothers who have a child while on welfare. This argument is increasingly advanced by members of the Republican Party and is a reform proposal adopted by several states (see chapter 6).

In summary, low wages and high rates of unemployment for low-skill males, especially minorities; the independence provided women by their careers; a more liberal public attitude about single parenting; and the availability of welfare all contribute to some extent to the major increases in divorce and out-of-wedlock births that have taken place over the last thirty years.

Why Are Mother-Only Families So Poor?

There is general agreement that mother-only families suffer high rates of poverty for three major reasons. Each is discussed below.

Lack of Adequate Child Support

One of the most obvious factors contributing to the poverty of mother-only families is the low level of child support by absent fathers (Bureau of the Census 1994a, Table 604). In recent years only about half of all women with minor children from an absent father have been awarded child support, and of these, only about half have received the agreed-upon amount (Table 3.4). Figures for 1989 provide examples from a typical year. In 1989 there were 9.9 million women with children from an absent father. Exactly 50 percent of these women won court decisions ordering the absent father to make support payments. However, only three-quarters of those awarded support ever received any money, and of those who did only 51 percent received the full amount. The mean payments received by mothers was $2,995. Thus, most mothers did not receive any support, and those who did tended to receive rather modest amounts.

White women generally receive more support than do minor-

Table 3.4

Women Seeking Child Support Payments by Race, 1989

Race	Numbers (in millions)	Percentage awarded payments	Percentage receiving payments	Mean annual support
All women	9.9	50.0	75.0	$2,995
White	6.9	58.0	77.0	3,132
Black	2.8	28.5	70.0	2,263
Hispanic	1.1	33.0	70.0	2,965
Women below poverty level seeking support				
All women	3.2	37.0	68.0	$1,889
White	1.7	47.0	68.0	1,972
Black	1.3	25.0	70.0	1,674
Hispanic	.536	28.0	64.0	1,824

Source: Bureau of the Census 1994a, Tables 604 and 605.

ity women. The data in Table 3.4 suggest considerable variance in support by race. None of the family types received decent levels of financial support, but white women were more often awarded support and were more likely to receive the support awarded. Only 28.5 percent of black women were awarded payments, and only 70 percent of those families received any funds. The situation was little better for Hispanic women. Minority women fare worse in part because they have a higher out-of-wedlock birth rate and paternity is established in fewer than one-third of these cases (Nichols-Casebolt and Garfinkel 1991). Additionally, eight of ten divorced mothers are awarded support compared to only three in ten unmarried mothers. But even among divorced mothers, postdivorce income plummets to about 60 percent of predivorce income (Holden and Smock 1991; Duncan and Hoffman 1988).

Women below the poverty level are even less likely to be awarded or to receive child support. Only 37 percent of all women living in poverty were awarded support and only 68 percent of those families received any payments in 1989. Black and

Hispanic mothers were even less likely to be awarded support or to benefit from payments. Among all poor women the mean annual dollars received was only $1,889.

The low level of financial support by minority men obviously has a financial antecedent. Several studies have shown that low-income black males have conventional attitudes toward marriage and family life, but high rates of unemployment and limited income make it difficult for them to be stable providers and marriage partners (Levy 1980, 42–46; Ross and Sawhill 1975, 74, 86).

Women's Income

The economic condition of female household heads is also affected by a series of problems related to employment and wage earnings (Chafetz 1984, 47–79). Most obviously, unemployment rates for female family heads are very high. In 1992 only about 40 percent of all women heading a household with children under 18 and having no spouse present worked full-time year-round (Bureau of the Census 1995, 32). By race the rate was 42 percent for white, 35 percent for black, and 30 percent for Hispanic families.

Studies conducted at the University of Wisconsin's Institute for Research on Poverty demonstrated how significantly unemployment rates impact on poor families. The studies revealed that a 10 percent increase in the unemployment rate is associated with about a 2.5 percent increase in the incidence of pretransfer (before government transfers) poverty. Thus, if unemployment increased from 9 to 10 percent, the number of families with earnings below the poverty level would increase from 20 percent to 20.5 percent, adding over a million new people to the ranks of the poor (U.S. House 1984b, 63).

Even when women are employed, they tend to earn less than male workers. In 1993 the median income for women working full-time year-round was $22,469, compared to $31,077 for males. Similarly, female family heads had a median income from all sources (i.e., wages, welfare benefits, and child support) of $17,443, compared to $43,005 for married-couple families (Bureau of the Census 1995, Table 3).

Women workers earn significantly less than male workers for several reasons (Bergman 1989; Fuchs 1989). Many more women work only part-time or part of the year. Women also tend to change jobs and move in and out of the work force more often. Among full-time workers the discrepancy between male and female wages is caused by many factors. First, the mean age of working women is considerably younger than that of male employees (which means that women tend to have less seniority). Second, women employees tend to be concentrated in jobs traditionally considered "women's work," and these jobs usually pay a rather low wage regardless of the skill and training required. Third, there is solid empirical evidence of pay discrimination as recently as the 1970s, and some discrimination may continue (see Bergman 1974; Cocoran and Duncan 1979; Lloyd and Niemi 1979; Suter and Miller 1973; Wolf and Fligstein 1979).

The economic condition of all American families has also been affected over the last twenty years by the failure of wages to keep up with inflation. Adjusted for inflation, the median income for all families in 1970 was $33,519. By 1993 median family income had only risen to $36,959 (Bureau of the Census 1995, Table 3). The median income of white families increased very modestly over this period, but wages were stagnant for black and Hispanic families. Family incomes have been influenced by the increase in female-headed families, the loss of many well-paying industrial-manufacturing jobs, the increase in the proportion of jobs in lower-paying service sectors, and the increase in involuntary part-time work (Danziger and Gottschalk 1988–1989; Danziger, Gottschalk, and Smolensky 1989).

Inadequate Social Welfare Programs

Despite the fact that the dramatic growth in mother-only families is one of the most important demographic changes in the latter half of the twentieth century, public policy has not been adequately altered to accommodate or deal with the reality of this massive change in the American family. The result is that when millions of mother-only families fall below the poverty level, existing social welfare programs neither help significant numbers of them escape poverty nor play a preventive role in reducing the increasing frequency of new mother-only families. These issues will be discussed in more detail in chapters 4 and 6.

Interestingly, as the number of mother-only families and poverty among American children have increased, welfare benefits in inflation-adjusted dollars have declined. In analyzing the Aid to Families with Dependent Children (AFDC) program, Blank (1994, 179) found: "In 1992 dollars, median benefits were at a high of $761 per month in 1970 and fell to a low of $435 per month by 1992, a decline of 43 percent." Benefits declined in part because welfare caseloads have increased, the percentage of all American families led by mother-only families has continued, and strains on both the federal and state budgets have become more severe. Thus, more families are getting benefits, but stipends are lower, leaving most recipients below the poverty level and the problems that made them poor unaddressed.

Conclusions

For the foreseeable future, a significant proportion of all American families will probably be headed by a single woman, many of whom will be mothers of dependent children. While the welfare reform proposals discussed in chapter 6 may place some degree of emphasis on reducing out-of-wedlock births, it is not clear how effective these policies will be even if adopted, especially in the short run. Divorce rates will probably be impacted even less by public policies. Thus, it seems realistic to conclude that over the next couple of decades, American society will have a significant stake in the health and well-being of the large number of citizens who live in mother-only families. Effective social and welfare policies will have to deal with those factors that contribute to the creation of mother-only families and those factors that leave such a large percentage of them in a state of poverty.

In this chapter we have identified some of the major factors that create mother-only families and the reasons such a large percentage of these families are poor. In the next chapter we will examine America's major welfare programs to determine how responsive they are to the factors identified and to reflect upon the implications for welfare reform.

Chapter 4

The Social Welfare Response

Of all the major Western industrial nations, the United States has always been the most conservative about social welfare policy. America's welfare programs are the most recent in origin and the most limited in design, coverage, and cost among the major Western powers (OECD 1976; Smeeding 1992; Wilensky 1975, 11). Despite their relative modesty, American welfare programs rest on tentative public support (Feagin 1975; Shapiro, Patterson, Russell, and Young 1987). The American public is very sympathetic toward the poor, but does not much like welfare and does not want social policy to be wasteful or to reward, support, or encourage indolence or immoral behavior. There is always a concern that welfare programs have these flaws and consequences (Bobo and Smith 1994).

The Historical Context

Decades after the other major Western industrial nations had begun developing welfare programs, the United States established its first: very limited and modest programs in response to the Great Depression, which began in 1929 (Katz 1986; Piven and Cloward 1971, 1979). The economic collapse brought about by the depression was so massive that by 1933 one-fourth of the nation's adult men were unemployed, millions of families were losing their homes, and thousands stood in bread lines each day. Millions of those who suffered from the economic crisis had formerly been solid members of America's middle class (Rodgers 1979, 43–72). Still, the government's response to the crisis was cautious and slow. Between 1933 and 1935, President Franklin D. Roosevelt centered his attention primarily on emergency measures such as public works projects and prevention of bank closures.

By 1935 the crisis had worsened. The Works Progress Administration (WPA) provided jobs for millions of U.S. citizens, but some 8 million males were still unemployed. It has been estimated that the WPA provided jobs to only one of every four applicants (Piven and Cloward 1971, 98). Those millions who could not find work, along with the aged, the handicapped, and orphans, turned to state and local governments for assistance. Many states, however, could not handle the burden. Some cut the size of grants so that more of the needy could receive some assistance; others abolished all assistance. New Jersey offered the indigent licenses to beg (Piven and Cloward 1971, 109).

The Social Security Act of 1935

The continuing hardship spawned increasing criticism of the Roosevelt administration. Under these pressures, the president launched what historians refer to as the "second New Deal." This New Deal had three primary thrusts. First, the government would use Keynesian economics to stimulate and, it was hoped, regulate and moderate economic cycles. Second, assistance to business was increased in hopes of promoting an economic recovery. Third, to assist many of those impoverished by the depression, Congress established, through the Social Security Act of 1935, assistance programs for those who were outside the labor force.

The Social Security Act consisted of five major titles:

Title I provided grants to the states for assistance to the aged;

Title II established the Social Security system;

Title III provided grants to the states for the administration of unemployment compensation;

Title IV established the Aid to Dependent Children (ADC) program;

Title V provided grants to the states for aid to the blind and disabled.

The Social Security Act created a new role for the federal government, which at the time was quite radical. Congress previously had subsidized state and local assistance programs, but this was the first time programs had been established that would be run by the federal government (Social Security) or in partnership with the states (ADC).

As fundamental a departure as the Social Security Act was, its benefits were originally quite modest. Grants under Social Security were extended only to those aged who worked in certain occupations and industries, and payments were delayed until 1942. It was not until 1950 that half the aged received any benefits under the program. ADC was sold as a program for widows and their dependent children, and until 1950 only orphans and poor children received assistance. In 1950 the program was changed to Aid to Families with Dependent Children (AFDC), allowing benefits to one parent (normally the mother) in a family with eligible children.

With the passage of the Social Security Act of 1935, the United States became the last major industrial nation to develop a national welfare program—one that was by European standards quite modest. Three features of the act had long-term and significant consequences for U.S. social welfare programs. First, benefits under the various Social Security titles were designed for only a select category of the needy rather than all the poor. Even as social welfare programs expanded greatly in the 1960s and early 1970s, they continued to be categorical rather than universal, as they are in many other nations. The implications of this design feature will be examined in more detail in chapter 5.

Second, some of the Social Security titles allowed the states to determine who would receive assistance and how much they would receive. This meant that America would not have a uniform welfare program. As AFDC expanded to become the nation's primary cash assistance program for the needy, this feature remained. As will be detailed below, variations in state participation and payments under AFDC are huge, with some states providing much more generous assistance than others. Titles I and V also allowed a great deal of local autonomy in funding assistance to the aged and blind. Until these titles were superseded in 1974 by the Supplemental Security Income (SSI) program, funding variations by state were substantial.

Last, the Social Security Act did not include health insurance. By 1935 most other Western industrial nations already had health insurance programs. Roosevelt considered including health insurance in the Social Security Act but eliminated it because opposition from the American Medical Association and southern congressmen was so intense.

State control over the benefit levels under Titles I, II, IV, and V of the Social Security Act substantially limited growth in these programs through the 1950s. In 1960 only 803,000 families were receiving benefits under AFDC, and only 144,000 blind or disabled citizens were receiving assistance under Title V. Thus, by 1960, twenty-five years after the original act, U.S. welfare programs were still extremely modest, and, as events would prove, poverty was very severe.

The Civil Rights Movement

Just as the Great Depression had served as the necessary catalyst for the nation's first major social welfare programs, the civil rights movement and the ghetto riots of the 1960s served as the stimulus for the next substantial expansion of the welfare state. The civil rights movement, which matured in the late 1950s and early 1960s, focused attention on the economic conditions of millions of U.S. citizens. Civil rights workers often charged that many U.S. citizens of all races were ill-housed, ill-clothed, medically neglected, malnourished, and even suffering from hunger. Most of the nation's public leaders simply dismissed the latter suggestion, but slowly the evidence of acute poverty, malnutrition, and poverty-related diseases began to be documented.

In 1967 the Senate Subcommittee on Employment, Manpower, and Poverty held hearings on U.S. poverty. The testimony of many civil rights leaders contained graphic allegations of acute poverty and hunger in the South. Again, these charges were largely dismissed, but the testimony stimulated two liberal members of the subcommittee—Robert Kennedy (D., N.Y.) and Joseph Clark (D., Pa.)—personally to tour the Mississippi Delta. The tour turned into a major media event that documented severe hunger and malnutrition among Mississippi's poor.

The subcommittee's initial investigation also encouraged the Field Foundation to send a team of doctors to Mississippi to investigate the health of children in Head Start programs. The team issued a report documenting extensive poverty, poverty-related diseases, and malnutrition among the children and their families (Kotz 1971, 8–9).

The most dramatic documentation of U.S. poverty was yet to come. In the mid-1960s the Field Foundation and the Citizens' Crusade Against Poverty formed the Citizens' Board of Inquiry into Hunger and Malnutrition in the United States. After hundreds of on-site investigations and hearings, the Citizens' Board reported its findings in late 1967 and 1968. The findings confirmed the worst suspicions of welfare reform advocates. Investigators had discovered, within the larger population of the United States, a population that might best be described as an underdeveloped nation. They reported "concrete evidence of chronic hunger and malnutrition in every part of the United States where we have held hearings or conducted field trips" (Citizens' Board of Inquiry 1968, iv).

These findings contributed powerfully to pressures on Congress for improvements in and expansion of welfare programs. As leaders of the civil rights movement lobbied for assistance for the poor, their arguments were bolstered by the outbreak of hundreds of riots in U.S. cities between 1965 and 1969 (Downes 1968). Many saw the riots as evidence of a breakdown of morals in American society and an attack on the nation's institutions (Hahn and Feagin 1970). In the final analysis, however, most members of Congress agreed that expanding social programs would lower tensions and help restore order. Thus, with the cities on fire and media attention focused on the struggles of the black population and the poverty of millions of U.S. citizens, Congress passed major civil rights acts in 1964, 1965, and 1968. It also expanded existing welfare programs and created new ones. The changes included:

1. a 1961 amendment to the AFDC title, allowing states to provide benefits to families where both parents were unemployed (less than half the states adopted this option);
2. formal establishment of the Food Stamp program in 1964 (initially, only twenty-two states opted to participate);
3. enactment of the Medicare and Medicaid programs in 1965;
4. adoption by Congress in 1971 of national standards for the Food Stamp program (the program was not extended to all states until 1974);
5. passage of the Supplemental Security Income (SSI) program in 1972, effective in 1974.

By 1975 five new titles had been added to the Social Security Act, and the original titles had been expanded through amendments. The 1960s and early 1970s, then, saw the second significant installment in the development of American social welfare programs. It is doubtful that anything short of serious civil strife could have produced such drastic changes.

Still, American welfare programs retain much of the design initially imposed by the Social Security Act of 1935 and they are basically conservative. Assistance has remained categorical (often only specific groups among the poor are given aid), aid is given more like charity than in the universal forms popular in

Europe, and assistance is generally given only after a person becomes poor, not before. One result is that most of the money spent on welfare is designed to confront the symptoms of poverty, rather than its causes. Also, as we will see, especially among mother-only families, benefits are so modest that they leave the vast majority of recipient families in poverty. And, last, a large percentage of the poor receive no assistance because they do not fit into one of the categories of poor who are deemed to be legitimate or "truly needy."

With an understanding that welfare programs for mother-only families fit within this context, we can examine and critique existing programs.

Welfare Programs for Mother-Only Families

In one sense mother-only families with children are fortunate because they are among the categories of people—along with the aged, disabled, and blind—who are usually considered the "legitimate" poor under current welfare programs. Consequently, if they fall below federal and state income and asset levels, these families can generally qualify for one or more assistance programs. Impoverished nonaged single adults (especially males), nonaged couples (especially those without children), and male-headed families generally find it difficult to qualify for assistance, except food stamps and in some states general assistance and/or medical assistance. As we will detail below, the Family Support Act of 1988 increased the eligibility of two-parent families for AFDC, but the vast majority of recipients are still members of mother-only families. In fact, mother-only families with dependent children receive the majority of funds expended by the federal government for means-tested programs.

Impoverished mother-only families may qualify for benefits from several types of programs. Table 4.1 provides an overview of the nation's major social welfare programs, including expenditures for recent years. The programs can be divided into three types:

Table 4.1

Federal and State Expenditures for Selected Welfare Programs (in millions of dollars)

	1980	1981	1982	1983	1984	1985	1986	1987	1988	1989	1990	1991	1992	1993
Social Insurance														
Social Security	103.5	145.0	154.1	158.3	173.6	183.9	193.8	202.4	213.9	227.1	243.3	263.1	281.6	298.2
Unemployment compensation	18.9	19.6	23.8	25.3	13.6	14.4	16.0	14.4	13.2	16.4	20.0	31.3	37.3	34.1
Medicare	35.0	42.4	50.5	56.9	62.5	71.4	75.9	81.6	87.7	96.5	109.7	116.6	132.2	145.8
Cash Assistance														
AFDC	11.5	7.9	8.0	13.8	14.5	14.6	15.2	16.0	16.6	17.4	18.5	20.3	22.3	22.3
SSI	7.9	8.6	9.0	9.4	10.4	11.1	12.1	12.9	14.4	14.7	16.1	18.0	21.2	24.2
In-Kind Programs														
Medicaid	25.8	30.4	32.4	34.9	37.5	40.9	44.8	49.3	54.1	61.2	72.5	91.5	118.2	132.0
Food stamps	9.2	11.3	11.1	12.7	12.5	12.6	12.5	12.5	13.3	13.8	16.5	19.7	23.5	24.8
Head Start	735.0	818.7	911.7	912.0	995.8	1.1	1.04	1.13	1.2	1.2	1.5	1.9	2.2	2.8
WIC	724.7	874.4	948.2	1.1	1.4	1.5	1.6	1.7	1.8	1.9	2.1	2.3	2.5	2.8
School lunch program	3.0	2.9	2.6	2.8	2.9	3.0	3.2	3.4	3.4	3.5	3.7	4.1	4.5	4.7

Source: U.S. House 1994 (*Green Book*): 176, 262, 264, 325, 761, 796–797, 829, 835.

1. Social insurance programs such as Social Security, Medicare, and unemployment compensation. Social insurance programs are based on employee and/or employer contributions, and benefits are wage-related.
2. Cash-assistance programs such as Aid to Families with Dependent Children (AFDC) and Supplemental Security Income (SSI). These programs are means-tested, with benefits going only to those who meet income and other qualifications.
3. In-kind programs such as food stamps and other nutrition programs, Medicaid, and Head Start, which provide a non-cash service. These programs are also means-tested and often have nonincome-related qualifications that must be met by recipients.

As the figures in Table 4.1 make clear, the three social insurance programs are collectively by far the most expensive of all social welfare programs. Strictly speaking, they are not welfare programs because recipients contribute to them during their working years and receive benefits related to contributions. Mother-only families may receive benefits from these programs as a result of retirement, unemployment, or disability or as spouses and children of workers with earned coverage.

The two means-tested cash assistance programs are designed for the poor. In fiscal 1993, AFDC and SSI cost the federal and state governments $22.3 billion and $24.2 billion, respectively. The in-kind programs are also designed for the poor. The most costly is Medicaid, a health program for the indigent. In 1993 the total cost of this program was $132 billion, more than two and a half times the combined annual cost of AFDC, Food Stamps, and Head Start. The vast majority of all social welfare spending is for Social Security, Medicare, and Medicaid. The programs that most directly serve the poor, and attract the most attention and concern, AFDC and Food Stamps, have a combined cost of only about 3 percent of the total cost of all social welfare programs.

Table 4.2 shows who received welfare benefits in 1992. Members of female-headed families constituted about 14 percent of

Table 4.2

Program Participation Status of Households by Poverty Status of Persons, 1992 (numbers in thousands)

Characteristic	Total	In household that received means-tested assistance		In household that received means-tested assistance excluding school lunches		In household that received means-tested cash assistance		In household that received food stamps		In household in which one or more persons are covered by Medicaid		Live in public or subsidized housing	
		Number	%	Number	%	Number	%	Number	%	Number	%	Number	%
All income levels													
Total	253,969	61,165	24.1	50,355	19.8	28,101	11.1	27,620	10.9	40,364	15.9	10,567	4.2
65 years and older	30,870	5,602	18.1	5,505	17.8	3,009	9.7	1,537	5.0	3,753	12.2	1,489	4.8
In families	215,515	53,405	24.8	43,017	20.0	24,379	11.3	24,134	11.2	35,396	16.4	8,303	3.9
Related children under 18 years	65,691	23,659	36.0	18,327	27.9	10,594	16.1	12,317	18.7	15,554	23.7	4,273	6.5
In married-couple families	171,514	30,087	17.5	22,645	13.2	10,563	6.2	10,028	5.8	17,954	10.5	2,270	1.3
Related children under 18 years	48,532	12,032	24.8	8,295	17.1	3,572	7.4	4,432	9.1	6,755	13.9	865	1.8

In families with female householder, no spouse present	35,639	20,580	57.7	18,044	50.6	12,455	34.9	12,863	36.1	15,473	43.4	5,775	16.2
Related children under 18 years	14,801	10,583	71.5	9,205	62.2	6,534	44.1	7,337	49.6	8,059	54.4	3,288	22.2
Unrelated individuals	34,734	6,746	18.4	6,510	17.7	3,211	8.7	2,922	8.0	4,219	11.5	2,171	5.9
Below poverty level													
Total	36,880	26,980	73.2	24,552	66.6	15,735	42.7	18,930	51.3	20,790	56.4	6,794	18.4
65 years and older	3,983	1,873	47.0	1,847	46.4	1,051	26.4	932	23.4	1,348	33.8	611	15.3
In families	27,947	22,637	81.0	20,349	72.8	13,276	47.5	16,449	58.9	17,626	63.1	5,606	20.1
Related children under 18 years	13,876	12,262	88.4	11,051	79.6	7,491	54.0	9,326	67.2	9,756	70.3	3,302	23.8
In married-couple families	12,830	9,193	71.7	7,717	60.1	3,732	29.1	5,773	45.0	6,342	49.4	1,019	7.9
Related children under 18 years	5,268	4,306	81.7	3,555	67.5	1,677	31.8	2,778	52.7	2,963	56.2	479	9.1
In families with female householder, no spouse present	13,716	12,408	90.5	11,727	85.5	8,952	65.3	10,017	73.0	10,464	76.3	4,431	32.3
Related children under 18 years	8,032	7,484	93.2	7,090	88.3	5,534	68.9	6,229	77.6	6,418	79.9	2,735	34.1
Unrelated individuals	7,991	3,613	45.2	3,563	44.6	2,037	25.5	2,026	25.4	2,567	32.1	1,106	13.8

Source: Bureau of the Census 1993.

the American population, but they were the major welfare recipient group. Excluding the elderly population, persons in female-headed families constituted 49 percent of all recipients of food stamps, 63 percent of those persons living in subsidized housing, 42 percent of all persons who were served by Medicaid, and 50 percent of those persons receiving cash assistance from the government, which includes everything from AFDC to assistance with college loans.

Almost 58 percent of all persons living in female-headed families received means-tested assistance (meaning they were qualified by low income and assets), rising to 71.5 percent if the family contained children under eighteen. As we will detail below, AFDC families almost always receive benefits from more than one program. An AFDC family generally receives food stamps, Medicaid, and free or reduced-price school meals, and they may receive some type of training along with other services such as housing assistance. Mother-only families, then, are usually not viable economic units; most require public assistance, more so than any other family type.

Table 4.3 provides a broad overview of the effectiveness of social welfare programs in reducing poverty. In 1992, for example, over 22 percent of the American population (57 million people) would have been poor if there had been no social welfare programs. After receipt of social welfare benefits including cash, food, and housing, the poverty count was reduced to about 13 percent of all Americans, some 33 million people. The programs that prevent the largest number of people from being poor are the social insurance programs, especially Social Security and SSI. These programs prevent about 30 percent of all recipients from living below the poverty line. Means-tested cash, food, and housing programs are less effective, lifting about 12 percent above the poverty level. Combined, the programs reduced the pretransfer poverty population by nearly 42 percent, a very substantial decrease in the poverty population.

Table 4.3 also shows that 16.5 percent of those families receiving cash, food, and housing assistance were removed from

Table 4.3

Antipoverty Effectiveness of Cash and Noncash Transfers for All Persons (Including Federal Income and Payroll Taxes) (in thousands)

	1979	1983	1989	1990	1991	1992
Total population	222,893	231,140	246,492	248,054	251,179	253,969
Number of poor individuals						
Cash income before transfers	42,783	52,700	49,052	50,851	54,679	57,021
Plus social insurance (other than Social Security)	40,867	49,468	47,377	49,052	52,164	54,367
Plus Social Security	28,604	36,928	33,825	35,928	38,131	39,717
Plus means-tested cash transfers	25,924	35,030	31,534	33,585	35,708	36,880
Plus food and housing benefits	21,546	31,697	27,642	29,377	31,129	32,680
Less federal taxes	22,215	33,923	28,941	30,465	31,770	33,118
Number of individuals removed from poverty due to						
Social insurance (other than Social Security)	1,916	3,232	1,675	1,799	2,515	2,654
Social insurance (including Social Security)	14,179	15,772	15,227	14,923	16,548	17,304
Means-tested cash, food, and housing benefits	7,058	5,231	6,183	6,551	7,002	7,037
Federal taxes	−669	−2,226	−1,299	−1,088	−641	−438
Total	20,568	18,777	20,111	20,386	22,909	23,903
Percent of poor individuals removed from poverty due to						
Social insurance (including Social Security)	33.1	29.9	31.0	29.3	30.3	30.3
Means-tested cash, food, and housing benefits	16.5	9.9	12.6	12.9	12.8	12.3
Federal taxes	−1.6	−4.2	−2.6	−2.1	−1.2	−0.8
Total	48.1	35.6	41.0	40.1	41.9	41.9

Source: U.S. House 1994 (*Green Book*): 1171.

poverty in 1979, but only some 12 percent were moved above the poverty line in 1992. Welfare programs are becoming less effective. This is an important insight and one that will be detailed below. The effectiveness of welfare programs is declining in part because the poverty population increasingly includes a larger percentage of mother-only families, a family type that is both particularly poor and more difficult to help. Another reason is that federal and state spending on welfare programs has failed to keep pace with inflation, thus declining in real dollars. In the 1960s and about halfway through the 1970s, spending on welfare increased substantially. By the end of the 1970s real-dollar increases halted, and in the early 1980s welfare spending came under serious attack. The reductions in real expenditures declined because the economy faltered and because conservatives raised serious questions about the impact and effectiveness of welfare programs (Murray 1984).

President Reagan launched a serious attack on welfare spending (Congressional Budget Office [CBO] 1983; Danziger 1982; Danziger and Haveman 1981; Gottschalk 1981; Moffitt and Wolf 1987; U.S. House 1984a, 80). When Reagan's massive tax cuts and huge defense expenditures created a serious revenue shortfall and thus huge deficits, the president convinced Congress that welfare programs had to be cut (Tobin 1994, 165). Eligibility standards were tightened and funding for many programs was reduced. Between 1980 and 1985, some 4 million people were dropped from means-tested programs. Three million people were dropped from the Food Stamp rolls, while 95 percent of those remaining eligible had their benefits reduced. Some 350,000 families, including 1.5 million children, lost AFDC benefits. Thirty-six states dropped mothers of three with earnings of $5,000 a year or more. Thirteen states set the cutoff level for families of four at $3,000. Three million children lost their eligibility for the school lunch program; almost one million women and children lost their Medicaid coverage.

A congressional study found that real expenditures (adjusted for inflation) for poor children and their guardians dropped substantially between 1973 and 1983 (U.S. House 1985a, 177). Despite the fact that the number of poor children increased by over 30 percent during this period, expenditures, adjusted for inflation, dropped about 6 percent. Funding for all means-tested programs dropped from 13.3 percent of the federal budget in 1980 to about 9 percent in 1988. This represented a decline of about a third in the share of the federal budget going to low-income programs.

By the beginning of the 1990s, welfare spending was again increasing and caseloads were at record levels, but both major political parties were questioning the size, impact, and wisdom of the nation's major welfare programs. As we will detail in chapter 6, the mid- to late 1990s are likely to be an era of major welfare reform. The program that is most likely to be the focus of attention and reform is AFDC.

Aid to Families with Dependent Children

The core cash-welfare program for poor families is AFDC. All states plus the District of Columbia, Puerto Rico, Guam, and the Virgin Islands participate in the AFDC program. Over most of its history, AFDC has been a program for one-parent families with children below the poverty level. Until recently, states and other jurisdictions could provide at their option AFDC to some two-parent families under the AFDC-UP (Unemployed Parent) program. Twenty-six states chose to set up these programs. On October 1, 1990, the law changed to require all states to offer AFDC to children in two-parent families with incomes below the poverty level if the main wage earner is unemployed but has a work history. Those states that did not have an AFDC-UP program before the change in the law may limit benefits to as little as six months in any thirteen-month period. Despite the change in the law, in 1994 over 90 percent of AFDC families were headed by single women.

Table 4.4 provides an overview of the AFDC program, showing the increases in recipients and costs between 1970 and 1993.

Table 4.4

Summary of Key AFDC Program Elements (in dollars, except for caseloads)

	1970	1975	1980	1985	1988	1990	1991	1992	1993
Total AFDC									
Benefit expenditures (millions)	4,082	8,153	11,540	14,580	16,663	18,539	20,356	22,240	22,286
1993[a]	15,496	22,586	20,700	19,627	20,437	20,671	21,606	22,911	22,286
Federal share (millions)	2,187	4,625	6,448	7,817	9,125	10,149	11,165	12,252	12,270
1993[a]	8,303	12,813	11,566	10,523	11,192	11,316	11,850	12,621	12,270
Administrative cost (millions)	758	1,082	1,479	1,779	2,353	2,661	2,673	2,764	2,956
1993[a]	2,878	2,997	2,653	2,395	2,886	2,967	2,837	2,847	2,956
Federal share (millions)	572	552	750	890	1,194	1,358	1,373	1,422	1,518
1993[a]	2,171	1,529	1,345	1,198	1,464	1,514	1,457	1,465	1,518
Average monthly numbers (thousands)									
Families	1,909	3,269	3,574	3,692	3,748	3,974	4,375	4,769	4,981
All recipients	7,429	11,067	10,597	10,813	10,920	11,460	12,595	13,625	14,144
Children	5,494	7,821	7,220	7,165	7,326	7,755	8,515	9,225	9,539
Average family size	4.0	3.2	3.0	3.0	3.0	2.9	2.9	2.9	2.9
Average monthly benefit	178	208	269	329	370	389	388	389	373
per family 1993[a]	676	576	483	443	454	434	412	401	373

AFDC-Basic and AFDC-UP

Benefit expenditures (millions) 1993[a]									
Total AFDC	15,496	22,586	20,700	19,627	20,437	20,671	21,606	22,911	22,286
AFDC-Basic	14,620	21,583	19,457	17,532	18,695	19,021	19,667	20,728	19,990
AFDC-UP	877	1,003	1,243	2,095	1,742	1,650	1,939	2,183	2,298
Average monthly families (thousands)									
Total AFDC	1,909	3,269	3,574	3,692	3,748	3,974	4,375	4,769	4,981
AFDC-Basic	1,831	3,168	3,433	3,431	3,538	3,770	4,107	4,447	4,622
AFDC-UP	78	101	141	261	210	204	268	322	359
Average monthly benefit per family 1993[a]									
Total AFDC	676	576	483	443	454	434	412	401	373
AFDC-Basic	665	568	472	426	440	420	399	388	360
AFDC-UP	937	827	735	669	691	674	603	565	533

Source: Department of Health and Human Services, Administration for Children and Families, and Congressional Research Service. U.S. House 1994 (*Green Book*): 325.

Note: AFDC benefit expenditures have not been reduced by child support enforcement collections and do not include foster care payments; AFDC enrollment figures do not include foster care children.

[a]Adjusted for inflation using CPI-U (fiscal year).

The number of recipients almost doubled between 1970 and 1993 from 7.4 million to 14.1 million. The average size of AFDC families declined from 4 to 2.9 persons and the number of families more than doubled from 1.9 million to 5 million. The cost of the program increased substantially even in inflation-adjusted dollars (from $15.5 billion to $22.3 billion), but the increase in the caseload lowered benefits to the average recipient family. In 1993 dollars the average family received $676 in 1970 and only $373 in 1993, a 45 percent reduction.

In 1993 almost 5 million families participated in the AFDC program each month. Since the early 1970s, an average of about 70 percent of the recipients have been children. The primary reason children become eligible for AFDC is that their fathers are absent from home (about 87 percent) and their mothers cannot support them. In 1993 some 30 percent of fathers of AFDC families were absent because of divorce or separation, with another 53 percent absent because the mother had never married (U.S. House 1994, 401). The percentage of all AFDC families resulting from out-of-wedlock births increased from 27.9 percent in 1969 to over a majority of all AFDC families by 1988 (U.S. House 1994, 401). The huge increase in unwed mothers and their children is the most significant alteration in AFDC recipients in the history of the program.

Not only are never-married mothers and their children now the majority of AFDC recipients, substantially more AFDC families result from births to teenage mothers. Between 1976 and 1992 about 42 percent of all single women receiving AFDC were or had been teenage mothers. In 1992 about 5 percent of mother-only families on AFDC were headed by a teenager, while about 36 percent were headed by women who gave birth as a teenager (GAO 1994a, 8). Families started by teenagers are much more difficult to help because teen mothers tend to be less well educated than other AFDC mothers, to have poorer work histories, to earn less when they work, and to have larger families. As a consequence, families started by teens stay on welfare much longer than families that qualify for AFDC because of divorce or separation (GAO 1994b). It has been estimated that in 1990 the federal government spent about $25 billion supporting families begun by teenagers (GAO 1994a, 9).

Variations in AFDC Benefits

There are no standard cash benefits under the AFDC program. Each state determines the financial needs of its poor families and decides how much of that need to fund through AFDC. The federal government reimburses 50 to 78 percent of a state's AFDC costs (depending on the per-capita income of the state) and pays, on average, about 55 percent of all AFDC costs. The federal government sets maximum asset limits for recipients ($1,000), which states may lower. Homes, the equity value of a car up to $1,500 (or a lower state limit), and some items of personal property are generally not counted.

AFDC heads must report all income coming into the household, assign all awarded child support to the state, and cooperate with the state in establishing the paternity of each child in the family. By law the first $50 a month in child support received is not counted as income. Payments above this amount are assigned to the state. Some educational loans and grants are also not counted as income, and the earnings of dependent children are not counted as long as the dependent is a full-time student or is involved in certain job training programs. Despite these legal income disregards, if the gross income of the family exceeds 185 percent of the state's determined need level, the family cannot receive any AFDC benefits.

Table 4.5 shows how substantially the AFDC program varies by state. The states differ greatly in where they set the need level for families of various sizes, how much of that need they fund, the combined value of AFDC and food stamps, and how much of state need and the poverty level is met by combined benefits. A quick inspection of the table reveals that the differences are more substantial than variations in the cost of living. Maximum AFDC benefits for a three-person family varied from a low of $120 a month in Mississippi to a high of $923 a month in Alaska. Seven

Table 4.5

Gross Income Limit, Need Standard, and Maximum Monthly Potential Benefits in AFDC and Food Stamps for One-Parent Family of Three Persons, January 1994

State	Gross income limit (185% of need standard)	100% of "need"	Maximum AFDC grant[a]	Food stamp benefit[b]	Combined benefits	Combined benefits as a percentage of 1993 poverty threshold[c]	AFDC benefits as a percentage of 1993 poverty threshold[c]
Alabama	$1,245	$673	$164	$295	$459	48	17
Alaska	1,804	975	923	285	1,208	101	77
Arizona	1,783	964	347	292	639	67	36
Arkansas	1,304	705	204	295	499	52	21
California	1,323	715	607	214	821	86	63
Colorado	779	421	356	289	645	67	37
Connecticut	1,258	680	680	192	872	91	71
Delaware	625	338	338	295	633	66	35
District of Columbia	1,317	712	420	270	690	72	44
Florida	1,833	991	303	295	598	62	32
Georgia	784	424	280	295	575	60	29
Hawaii	2,109	1,140	712	422	1,134	103	65
Idaho	1,833	991	317	295	612	64	33
Illinois	1,647	890	367[d]	291	658	69	38
Indiana	592	320	288	295	583	61	30
Iowa	1,571	849	426	268	694	72	44
Kansas	794	429	429[d]	284	713	74	45
Kentucky	973	526	228	295	523	55	24

Louisiana	1,217	658	190	295	485	51	29
Maine	1,023	553	418	271	689	72	44
Maryland	938	507	366[d]	295	661	69	38
Massachusetts	1,071	579	579	222	801	83	60
Michigan							
Washtenaw County	1,086	587	489[d]	249	738	77	51
Wayne County	1,019	551	459[d]	258	717	75	48
Minnesota	984	532	532	236	768	80	55
Mississippi	681	368	120	295	415	43	13
Missouri	1,565	846	292	295	587	61	30
Montana	945	511	401	276	677	71	42
Nebraska	673	364	364	287	651	68	38
Nevada	1,293	699	348	292	640	67	36
New Hampshire	3,049	1,648	550	231	781	81	57
New Jersey	1,822	985	424[d]	276	700	73	44
New Mexico	660	357	357	289	646	67	37
New York							
Suffolk County	1,301	703[d]	703[d]	201	904	94	73
New York City	1,067	577	577[d]	239	816	85	60
North Carolina	1,006	544	272	295	567	59	28
North Dakota	757	409	409	273	682	71	43
Ohio	1,626	879	341[d]	295	636	66	36
Oklahoma	871	471	324	285	619	65	34
Oregon	851	460	460[d]	293	753	78	48
Pennsylvania	1,136	614	421	270	691	72	44
Rhode Island	1,025	554[d]	554[d]	268	822	86	58
South Carolina	814	440	200	295	495	52	21
South Dakota	908	491	417	271	688	72	43
Tennessee	788	426	185	295	480	50	19

(continued)

Table 4.5 (continued)

State	Gross income limit (185% of need standard)	100% of "need"	Maximum AFDC grant[a]	Food stamp benefit[b]	Combined benefits	Combined benefits as a percentage of 1993 poverty threshold[c]	AFDC benefits as a percentage of 1993 poverty threshold[c]
Texas	1,062	574	184	295	479	50	19
Utah	1,021	552	414	272	686	72	43
Vermont	2,079	1,124	638	205	843	88	67
Virginia	727	393	354	290	644	67	37
Washington	2,142	1,158	546[d]	258	804	84	57
West Virginia	919	497	249	295	544	57	26
Wisconsin	1,197	647	517	241	758	79	54
Wyoming	1,247	674	360	288	648	68	38
Guam	611	330	330	436	766	80	34
Puerto Rico	666	360	180	0	180	NA	19
Virgin Islands	555	300	240	380	620	65	25
Median AFDC State[e]	938	507	366	295	661	69	38

Source: Table prepared by CRS from information provided by a telephone survey of the states. U.S. House 1994 (Green Book): 366–367.

Notes: In most states these benefit amounts apply also to two-parent families of three (where the second parent is incapacitated or unemployed). Some, however, increase benefits for such families.

Puerto Rico does not have a Food Stamp program; instead, a cash nutritional assistance payment is given to recipients.

[a] In states with area differentials, figure shown is for area with highest benefit.

[b] Food Stamp benefits are based on maximum AFDC benefits shown and assume deductions of $338 monthly ($131 standard household deduction plus $207 maximum allowable deduction for excess shelter cost) in the forty-eight contiguous states and D.C. In the remaining four jurisdictions these maximum allowable food stamp deductions are assumed: Alaska, $582; Hawaii, $480; Guam, $513; and Virgin Islands, $267. If only the standard deduction were assumed, food stamp benefits would drop by about $62 monthly in most of the forty-eight contiguous states and D.C. Maximum food stamp benefits from October 1993 through September 1994 are $295 for a family of three except in these four jurisdictions, where they are as follows: Alaska, $388; Hawaii, $492; Guam, $436; and Virgin Islands, $380.

[c] Except for Alaska and Hawaii, this column is based on the Census Bureau's 1993 poverty threshold for a family of three persons, $11,521, converted to a monthly rate of $960. For Alaska, this threshold was increased by 25 percent; for Hawaii, by 15 percent.

[d] In these states part of the AFDC cash payment has been designated as energy aid and is disregarded by the state in calculating Food Stamp benefits. Illinois disregards $18; Kansas, $57; Maryland, $43; New Jersey, $25; New York, $53; Ohio, $14; Oregon, $118; Rhode Island, $127.85; Washington, $86.

[e] With respect to maximum AFDC benefit among 50 states and D.C.

southern states have set maximum benefit levels for a family of three below $225 per month, while twelve states have set maximum benefits at $500 or higher. The AFDC stipend across the nation for this family size averaged $366, or $122 per recipient. Except for about a third of the states, benefits are quite modest, and some states, mostly in the South, seem to make only a minimal attempt to aid their poor.

In recent years about 85 percent of all AFDC families have received food stamps (U.S. House 1994, 402). Food stamps are not counted in calculating AFDC benefits, but AFDC awards are considered in determining food stamp grants. The result is that food stamp grants are higher in states that pay the lowest average AFDC stipends, and this compensates in part for low cash grants. The Food Stamp program is a federal program with uniform eligibility and benefit standards across the nation. The program provides vouchers that are used by recipients to purchase food. The vouchers are as valuable as cash since AFDC mothers spend at least as much as the value of the stamps they receive on food (Blank 1994, 179).

Table 4.5 shows the combined value of AFDC and food stamps in each state and their value in relation to the 1993 poverty threshold for a family of three. The combined value averaged $661 nationally, varying from a low of $415 in Mississippi to a high of $1,208 in Alaska. On average, the combined value of AFDC and food stamps equaled 69 percent of the poverty level for these families. Only in Alaska and Hawaii are the combined maximum benefits enough to lift families over the poverty line. In many states, particularly southern states like Alabama, Mississippi, Tennessee, and Texas, families receiving maximum AFDC and food stamp benefits are left far below the poverty level.

Because the maximum combined benefits of AFDC and food stamps are on average modest and far below the poverty level, over 70 percent of all mother-only families participating in the program continue to live below the poverty level. Also, because of cutbacks, the percentage of all poor families with children receiving AFDC benefits has declined over the last decade. During the 1970s an average of 83 percent of all poor families with children under age eighteen received AFDC benefits; by 1992, only 69 percent received such assistance (U.S. House 1985a, 192; Bureau of the Census 1993, xviii). Similarly, during the 1970s an average of over 75 percent of all poor children received AFDC benefits. By 1983 only 53.3 percent were covered by the program (U.S. House 1985a, 212) and by 1992 the percentage was 63 (U.S. House 1994, 399).

There are a number of other programs that serve large numbers of AFDC families. AFDC families always qualify for Medicaid, a health care program that is extremely important to them, but, for obvious reasons, the benefits are not calculated as income. While on Medicaid the families' health care needs are covered without the payment of fees. As a work incentive, a family that leaves AFDC because earnings from employment push them over the poverty threshold continues to receive Medicaid coverage for twelve months. About 10 percent of all AFDC families also live in subsidized housing, and more than half the children in AFDC families receive free or reduced-price school meals (U.S. House 1994, 824).

The cumulative cost of maintaining AFDC families, then, is considerable. If a family receives AFDC, food stamps, Medicaid, free and/or reduced-price school meals, and subsidized housing, the combined cost can be substantial. Yet, most participant families continue to live in poverty, many for very long periods, and the problems that have made them poor may never be addressed. Millions of other poor women and children, for one reason or another, are never served by AFDC.

The Child Support Enforcement Program

To reduce public outlays for women and children, the federal government over the last twenty years has invested increased effort in identifying absent parents and requiring them to contribute to the financial needs of their children. The intent has been both to improve the financial situation of the custodial parent and children and to reduce the need for and cost of public programs such as AFDC. The Social Security Act requires all states to establish a Child Support Enforcement (CSE) program to assist custodial parents of all income levels in obtaining child support. Amendments in 1975 and the Family Assistance Act of 1988 significantly expanded and strengthened state program and performance standards and provided federal matching dollars to help run the programs. All AFDC applicants and recipients must assign their child-support rights over to the states. Applicants and recipients must also cooperate with the state in obtaining financial support from an absent parent and, in cases where children are born out of wedlock, in establishing paternity.

Beginning in November 1990 the Family Support Act (FSA) required wage withholding of child support payments in all CSE enforcement cases. By January of 1994 the act required the states to provide wage withholding in all support orders issued after that date. The act also increased the authority of the states to garnishee wages, including military allotments; place liens on the property of delinquent parents; and collect from parents who cross state lines (U.S. House 1994, 477–489).

The determination to make both parents accept financial responsibility for their children has increased child support payments, and has reduced AFDC rolls and AFDC costs to some extent. The Office of Child Support Enforcement reported in 1993 that improved enforcement of child support had removed about 242,000 families from AFDC and reduced AFDC expenditures by 12 percent (U.S. House 1994, 455). In 1978 collections were made in only 458,000 AFDC cases. In 1993 collections rose to 873,000 cases. In nominal dollars, collections increased from $472 million in 1978 to $2.4 billion in 1993 (U.S. House 1994, 457).

While progress has been made, much remains to be done. In 1989 only about 43 percent of all poor mothers with dependent children were awarded child support. Only some 25 percent ever received any payments (U.S. House 1994, 463). Never-married mothers were the least likely to have the paternity of their children established, be awarded child support, or actually receive payments. As noted above, never-married mothers are an increasingly large proportion of all AFDC cases. Paternity is established in less than one-third of all cases where children are born to unwed mothers, and less than one-fourth of these mothers are awarded child support.

As is detailed in chapter 6, awarding and enforcing child support orders will be increasingly emphasized in reforms of AFDC. Both parents will be expected to accept responsibility for and support their children. As an antipoverty strategy, child support requirements might be most effective if they discourage men from fathering children they do not want to support. The amount of money that most low-income men can contribute will not move that many families off the welfare rolls. It has been estimated that noncustodial fathers have the financial potential to contribute about $27 billion a year to support their children. Yet, those children with fathers in the highest 20 percent of earners would receive 46 percent of the total while children with fathers in the lowest 20 percent of income earners would receive only 3 percent of all payments (U.S. House 1994, 501). Thus the poorest of noncustodial parents will not be able to make very substantial payments to help support their children.

AFDC Spells, Durations, and Exits

One reason that AFDC benefits are so modest is that the program is designed to be transitional, helping families for short periods while they get on their feet. Reality is more complex. Numerically, most recipients of AFDC receive benefits for a total of about four years (Moffitt 1992). This often includes more than one stay on AFDC (Bane and Ellwood 1994, 95–96). About 35 percent of all recipients leave the rolls only to return after losing a job or suffering another financial setback (Brandon 1995). Rather than transitional users, they are episodic users (Bane and Ellwood 1994, 41; Pavetti 1993). About half of all recipients remain on AFDC for more than four years, while about 25 percent remain on the rolls for ten years or more.

If the AFDC rolls are examined over a time period—a year, for example—the figures suggest that the average AFDC stay is short. But if the rolls are examined for any given day, the figures suggest that most AFDC families are long-term users. How can this be true? Imagine a hospital room with thirteen beds. Twelve beds are occupied by patients who will remain in the hospital for the full year. The thirteenth bed is occupied by a different patient each week. At the end of the year the hospital room has been used by sixty-four patients, and the average stay was short. But on any given day, 92 percent of the patients were long-term. This is the way AFDC works. The typical recipient uses AFDC short-term, but at any given time, the rolls are composed mostly of long-term users.

Bane and Ellwood (1994, 35–37) provide some important insights into the differences between long- and short-term users. The long-term users tend to be young, never-married mothers, especially those who drop out of high school and have little job experience. While only about 14 percent of divorced women remain on the rolls for ten or more years, about 40 percent of all never-married mothers do so (U.S. House 1994, 444). Bane and Ellwood also find that when AFDC recipients remain on the rolls for more than two years, they are in danger of becoming long-term users. On the other hand, when recipients manage to leave the rolls and stay off for at least three years, they usually do not return to AFDC (Hoynes and MaCurdy 1994).

Why do recipients leave AFDC? The largest number leave because they get married (35%). Another 11 percent leave because there are no longer any children in the household. Only 21 percent leave because the earnings of the female head increased (U.S. House 1994, 451).

AFDC Employment: Incentives and Disincentives

As originally designed, the intent of the program that has become AFDC was to provide funds to widows so that they could stay home with their children. Over time two things changed: (a) AFDC expanded to become a program that mostly enrolls divorced and unwed mothers; and (b) most women, including mothers, joined the work force. These changes have produced considerable interest in encouraging, even requiring, AFDC mothers to work. For the most part, all policy efforts have failed.

Beginning in 1967 the federal government required the states to establish Work Incentive Programs (WIN) to provide job search assistance and in some cases job training to work-eligible mothers with children over six. As an employment incentive for mothers, the law required the states to exclude the first $30 per month in earnings, one-third of all additional income, plus work expenses in calculating benefits. President Reagan was skeptical of the government's subsidizing people who worked. He wanted the law changed to require all able-bodied mothers to work in exchange for benefits and the income disregards amended. Compulsory work requirements were not passed by Congress but the earnings disregards were altered in 1982. Work expenses were capped at $75 per month and child care expenses were capped at $160 per month per child. The $30 and one-third disregard was limited to four consecutive months.

In 1984 the law was changed again. Congress mandated that states could not allow any family to receive AFDC if their gross income exceeded 185 percent of the state's need standard. Additionally, the $30 disregard was extended to eight months past the four-month rule for $30 and a third. Effective 1989, the law sets the work-expense monthly limit at $90, and at $175 for child care ($200 for children under two); requires that a child care disregard be calculated after all other disregards; and prohibits any benefits from the Earned Income Tax from being considered as income in calculating benefits.

The WIN program was primarily oriented toward helping AFDC mothers with job searches. The Family Support Act of 1988 (FSA) sought to alter this focus by requiring all states to replace WIN by establishing a job training and educational program for AFDC mothers by October 1, 1990. Under the Job Opportunities and Basic Skills (JOBS) training program, the states are required to enroll over time almost all able-bodied recipients with no children younger than three. Under JOBS, mothers are to be given the training and/or educational skills required to obtain employment and then be provided with transitional support while they become established in the work force. Medicaid benefits may be extended during the first year of employment along with child care assistance. This program is too recent to have had a major impact, but it signals a new approach to dealing with AFDC families. In chapter 6 the early assessments of state JOBS programs will be reviewed and evaluated.

Currently, very few AFDC mothers are employed. As Table 4.6 shows, employment of AFDC mothers has always been modest and the rates have declined over the last decade. In 1992 only 2.2 percent of all AFDC mothers held full-time jobs, while another 4.2 percent worked part-time. Why are so few AFDC mothers employed? First, there is the issue of child and health care. An AFDC mother cannot work unless she can either obtain help with child care costs or find a job that pays well enough to cover this very significant expense. Without job training or additional education, most AFDC mothers are not able to obtain jobs that pay much above the minimum wage. Additionally, if earnings from a job push a mother over the state income-qualification level, the family may lose both AFDC and Medicaid coverage. The Family Support Act provides that the states can provide transitional supportive health and child care assistance to parents who leave AFDC to work, but these benefits are soon exhausted.

Second, most AFDC mothers realize little financial gain by working. As noted above, in inflation-adjusted dollars AFDC benefits have declined significantly over the last couple of decades. This decline in benefits should give AFDC mothers an incentive to seek work rather than welfare. Yet, the alterations in disregards discussed above have made it less attractive for recipients to work. After four months recipients can no longer disregard one-third of their income and inflation had eroded much of the value of the $30 disregard. Table 4.6 shows the average AFDC earnings of mothers who work. In 1992 the average AFDC mother earned only $4,731, a significant decline from typical

Table 4.6

Employment and Earnings of AFDC Mothers

	May 1969	January 1973	May 1975	March 1979	1983	1986	1988	1990	1992
Mother's employment status (in percent)[a]									
Full-time job	8.2	9.8	10.4	8.7	1.5	1.6	2.2	2.5	2.2
Part-time job	6.3	6.3	5.7	5.4	3.4	4.2	4.2	4.2	4.2

	1976	1980	1984	1988	1992
Average earnings of AFDC mothers who work (1991 dollars)[b]	$7,161	$7,474	$4,455	$4,618	$4,731
Proportion of AFDC female-headed families with total income below 50% of poverty line (in percent)[c]	21.0	24.4	45.7	47.6	46.4
Average earnings of all AFDC mothers[d]					
Gave birth as teenager	$6,947	$6,347	$3,589	$4,082	$3,784
Did not give birth as teenager	$7,315	$8,374	$5,015	$4,871	$5,389

[a]U.S. House 1994 (*Green Book*): 402.
[b]GAO 1994c: 35.
[c]GAO 1994c: 39.
[d]GAO 1994c: 25.

earnings in the late 1970s and early 1980s. This decrease in earnings simply reflects the increasing shortage of jobs that pay low-skill workers well.

As Table 4.6 shows, AFDC mothers who gave birth as teenagers earn even less than the average. In 1992 these mothers earned only $3,784, compared to $5,389 for AFDC mothers who did not give birth as teens. Only about half of all teen mothers are high school graduates. They tend to have larger families, and they usually have less work experience. This is important because, as noted above, an increasingly large percentage of all AFDC mothers gave birth out of wedlock while they were teens.

Child Care for AFDC Mothers

Unlike some of the other Western nations to be discussed in chapter 5, American governments have played a rather modest role in helping working families with child care. As more mothers have joined the labor force, increasing attention has been focused on whether the children of working parents are receiving proper care and whether governments should play a larger role in assuring that children's needs are being met (U.S. House 1994, 544). The needs of welfare families have been part of this larger debate. The Family Support Act of 1988 refocused AFDC toward helping recipient mothers obtain the education and job skills required to become independent. FSA was modestly funded and designed to be phased in over time, but its emphasis on helping mothers obtain the education and/or job training required to become both employed and independent will clearly be central to future reforms of AFDC (see chapter 6).

FSA included new child care programs for AFDC families and families in transition to independent employment. Additionally, in 1990 the Child Care and Development Block Grant and the At-Risk Child Care programs were enacted. These acts or amendments created four child care programs, three of which are for low-income families. The first program funds child care assistance for AFDC parents who are working or participating in approved education or job training programs. The second subsidizes transitional child care for AFDC families for limited periods (a maximum of twelve months) while they become established in the work force. The third funds child care for limited periods for families who are at risk of qualifying for AFDC unless they can become or stay employed.

Since these programs are recent, they are currently serving a rather small percentage of all actual or potential AFDC families. In 1992 only about 100,000 adults in JOBS education or training programs qualified for child care services. About 160,000 children in these families received child care (U.S. House 1994, 562, 565). Another 102,000 families received free or subsidized child care while they worked, were in transition, were at risk, or were in some type of non-JOBS education or training program (U.S. House 1994, 568).

Obviously, if the emphasis of future welfare reform is to place more actual or potential AFDC parents in education or job training programs, and support them while they become established in the work force, these programs will have to be greatly expanded.

Problems with the Current AFDC Program

As the major cash-assistance program for the poor in the United States, AFDC is fundamentally flawed. A very large percentage of all the nation's poor mothers and children are never served by the program. Of those who are, some 70 percent continue to live below the poverty level. The program plays no meaningful role in preventing poverty, nor does it ameliorate the problems of the overwhelming majority of families that come under its jurisdiction. Most families receive benefits from the program for a relatively short period of time, but about 20 percent of all recipients remain on the rolls for ten or more years. It is this group of recipients that compose most AFDC families on any given day and they are the group upon whom most AFDC funds are spent. Reforms in 1995 will allow the states to set time limits on AFDC recipients, and require compulsory work and education requirements of some recipients, but as we will discuss in chapter 6, this will be more complex than it might seem.

The Family Support Act of 1988 has altered the focus of AFDC in some very important ways. The emphasis on identifying and providing the educational and job training needs of AFDC mothers and then supporting them while they settle into the job market is positive. Unfortunately, only a very modest percentage of the 5 million families receiving AFDC are currently being served, but 1995 reforms may significantly expand these programs and services in many states (see chapter 6).

While there is no evidence that AFDC payments play a meaningful role in encouraging women to have children, there is increasing concern about extending welfare to teenage mothers. While only a very small percentage of all AFDC mothers are teenagers, a significant and growing percentage of all AFDC mothers gave birth as teenagers and often they first entered the AFDC rolls while in their teens. It is this group of recipients who tend to be long-term users of AFDC. To discourage births to unwed teenagers, reforms in 1995 may allow states to deny AFDC and other welfare benefits to teenage mothers.

As will be detailed in chapter 6, welfare reform measures being debated in Congress in late 1995 will give the states a great deal more discretion over their welfare programs. The Family Support Act will probably serve as the model for much state reform of AFDC. More recipients will be required to participate in education and job training programs; more recipients will be expected to leave the rolls within designated time periods; more recipients will be given transitional assistance while they become established in the job market. Teenage mothers may lose eligibility in many states.

Educational Programs for Low-Income Children

Not surprisingly, poor children generally are not high educational achievers (Snow et al. 1991; Murnane 1994). Researchers believe that poor achievement on the part of low-income children can be explained by lack of access to quality educational programs, as well as a stressful home environment and limited support from parents. The federal government finances about a dozen programs designed to provide poor, educationally deprived, or handicapped children with compensatory educational services (U.S. House 1984c, 115–155). Most of the funds subsidize programs run by public schools; there are special programs for Native Americans, for migrant children, and for bilingual education. Nationwide, only about a million poor and educationally deprived children receive preschool educational assistance, and some 5 million primary- and secondary-school students receive compensatory educational services each year, financed in whole or in part by federal revenues (Office of Technology Assessment 1992). Most of the student recipients are educationally deprived, but they are not necessarily officially poor. The federal government does not collect separate figures on educational assistance for poor children, but given the total number of students served, no more than 20 percent of all poor children could be receiving special educational services funded by the federal government.

Studies indicate that preschool programs for poor children can enhance their futures and return significant benefits to society. Well-designed experiments have proven that quality educational programs for preschoolers and their parents can produce meaningful educational gains, lower dropout rates, reduce teenage pregnancy, increase employment rates, and improve the chance that students will attend college or receive other types of advanced education (Berrueta-Clement et al. 1984; Schorr 1988; Barnett 1992). The best known of these experiments, including the Perry Preschool Program, involved enrolling poor children in intensive full-time, year-round educational programs. The teachers were highly skilled and specially trained for the experiment. Gramlich's (1986) evaluation of the Perry Preschool Program found that it not only produced excellent educational gains, but that it also more than paid for itself by reducing crime and welfare transfers, and by increasing the taxes paid by recipients.

Most federal expenditures for preschool programs go to Head

Start, a program that is not as sophisticated as the educational experiments mentioned above. Established in 1965, Head Start was initially hailed as the most innovative antipoverty strategy on the horizon. It was designed to improve the educational skills and nutritional and health care needs of poor children while providing education and social services to their parents. Initially the program was designed to serve 100,000 children during the summer of 1965, but enthusiasm was so high that 561,359 were enrolled, most in hastily assembled programs (Steiner 1976, 30).

Evaluations soon showed that most of the early summer programs were not effective. Certainly the initial expectation that a great deal could be accomplished in only one or two eight-week summer terms was unrealistic. Studies did show that the nutritional and health conditions of Head Start children tended to be considerably better than those of children from similar backgrounds who had not been in the program; but educational gains tended to be small, especially for children who had not participated in year-round programs (Mann 1977). The most critical of the studies, known as the Westinghouse Report, showed worthwhile gains for students in full-year programs, but only minor gains from the eight-week programs—gains that tended to fade as the child completed the first two years of public school (Cicirelli et al. 1977).

The negative reports convinced Congress to phase out most of the summer programs, a task largely accomplished by 1974 (U.S. House 1994, 885). The conversion to longer-term programs (mostly six to eight months) and experience-related innovations in teaching techniques led to improvements in Head Start's impact. More recent studies of Head Start show quite positive results (Berrueta-Clement et al. 1984; Yavis 1982, 21–34). After reviewing achievement studies in the early 1970s, Bernard Brown (1977, 9) of the Office of Child Development wrote that the studies provide "compelling evidence that early intervention works, that the adverse impact of a poverty environment on children can be overcome by appropriate treatment." The studies demonstrated that Head Start is very successful in cutting down the rate of school failure, in improving IQ scores and reading skills, and in helping children gain self-confidence. They suggested that the educational gains do not fade, and that a "sleeper effect" often showed up several years after program participation, with Head Start recipients proving more academically competent even into the junior high school years. The more exposure children had to Head Start, the more gains they made and maintained.

Despite the positive evaluations of Head Start over the last fifteen years, most programs could be significantly improved. Most Head Start programs still enroll children for only a few hours a day for six to eight months. The staff is generally not very well trained. While participants benefit from the program, the students tend to perform below the median level for all students. Educators recognize this gap as the next challenge that must be faced, and they point to inadequate funding and modest intervention as the primary reasons the programs do not have an even more positive impact.

Funding and enrollments in Head Start have remained rather modest, especially given the potential. Between 1982 and 1993 enrollments grew from 396,000 to over 700,000 children a year. By law 90 percent of the children in Head Start programs must be from poverty families. Even if the unlikely assumption is made that all students enrolled in Head Start in recent years were from poverty families, only about one-fifth of all those qualified for the program by their family's income have been served. This is true despite the fact that the increasingly positive evaluations of Head Start's impact have transformed it into one of Congress's more favored programs. While other social programs were being scaled back in recent years, Congress has continued to raise the appropriation for Head Start. In 1993 Congress allocated $2.8 billion for Head Start, triple the budget in 1984.

Given the potential for high-quality educational programs to improve the life chances of poor and low-income students, compensatory education should be a key feature of welfare reform.

The Women, Infants, and Children (WIC)
Food Program

The Supplemental Feeding Program for Women, Infants, and Children (WIC) established in 1972 has grown to be an important program for low-income and poor women and children. WIC provides supplemental food to low-income and poor pregnant and postpartum women and their infants and children below the age of five. Recipients must have incomes below 185 percent of the poverty level and be certified as nutritionally at risk by a health professional. Sometimes the families receive supplemental food but generally they are given vouchers that can be redeemed at retail outlets for specific food items required to meet their nutritional needs—for example, dairy products, cereals, fruits, and vegetables. In 1993 the average monthly benefit to each recipient was about $40 including administrative costs (U.S. House 1994, 827).

The WIC program served 5.9 million women, infants, and children in 1993, at a cost of $2.7 billion. This represented significant growth in the program over the last decade. In 1983, for example, 2.5 million women, infants, and children were served at a cost of $1.1 billion. It has been estimated that of those qualified by income for the program in recent years, because of budget limitations only about half have been served. About three-fourths of all recipients have incomes at or below the poverty level, and about 16 percent are AFDC recipients. The Congressional Budget Office recently estimated that if all eligible recipients could be funded, the program would serve 7.6 million women and children in fiscal 1994 (U.S. House 1994, 828).

There is evidence that WIC and other nutrition programs have had a very positive impact on the health of recipients. Evaluations of the WIC program credit it with reducing the number of children born with low birth weight, a condition linked to birth defects and increased probability of infant mortality (U.S. House 1985a, 260). There is also evidence that the Food Stamp program has had beneficial effects. In 1977 the Field Foundation sent a team of doctors into the nation's poorest counties to determine if the conditions of the poor had improved since the 1960s. The team reported very significant improvements in the nutrition and health of poor Americans. Most of the poor still lived in inadequate housing and still had far too few resources or opportunities for improvements, but unlike in the 1960s, they were much less often hungry and malnourished: "The facts of life for Americans living in poverty remain as dark or darker than they were ten years ago. But in the area of food there is a difference. The Food Stamp program, the nutritional component of Head Start, school lunch and breakfast programs, and to a lesser extent the Women-Infant-Children (WIC) feeding programs have made a difference" (Kotz 1979, 9). Or, as another Field Foundation doctor said, "Poverty is rampant but the Food Stamp program brings food into the most terrible situations" (Kotz 1979, 9). Despite improvements, there is still evidence of serious nutritional problems among America's poor (Korenman, Miller, and Sjaastad 1994).

Conclusions

The social welfare programs available to impoverished women and their children have grown considerably over the last thirty years, but they are seriously flawed. While millions of families receive much-needed assistance from the programs, individually and collectively the programs fail two important tests. They do a very poor job of preventing poverty among women and children and they fail to remediate the problems of the vast majority of those who receive benefits. This is true even of the overwhelming majority of the families who spend periods of ten or more years receiving AFDC, food stamps, and other benefits. For millions of AFDC families who simultaneously receive benefits from three to five welfare programs at considerable public expense, the families simply continue to live in poverty, often for very long periods. The typical AFDC family receives no educational or job training assistance, or even quality counseling. Children in AFDC families generally receive little or no special attention or help to improve their chances of being successful in education or employment. This is true despite the evidence that early education programs can be very effective.

The huge increase in mother-only families over the last thirty years, especially families resulting from births to unwed women, has swollen welfare rolls while exacerbating and highlighting the deficiencies of our major social welfare programs. As a percentage of all welfare recipients, never-married mothers and their children have grown enormously over recent years. Yet, welfare programs have played no role in discouraging births to unwed teens, and these programs have been particularly ineffective in helping these families escape welfare and lives of poverty. They are, in fact, the primary long-term recipients of welfare.

In chapter 6 we will examine reforms that hopefully could overcome the deficiencies of current programs.

Chapter 5

Social Welfare Lessons
from Europe

The major industrial nations of Western Europe have not eradi-
cated poverty, but their poverty rates are significantly lower than
the U.S. rate (Smeeding 1992; Smeeding and Rainwater 1991;
Wong, Garfinkel, and McLanahan 1993; Beckerman 1979; Commission of the European Communities 1981; OECD 1976). This
is especially true of the Scandinavian countries, Germany, Switzerland, Austria, Australia, the Netherlands, France, and the
United Kingdom (Smeeding 1992).

Table 5.1 compares the poverty rate in the United States to
rates in four European nations and Canada. Using a standardized
poverty definition and the most recent year in which comparable
data was available, Smeeding found that the American poverty
rate is about five times the rate in Germany, three times the rate
in Sweden and France, two and a half times the rate in the United
Kingdom, and almost double the Canadian rate. The United
States is the only nation with a double-digit rate of poverty. The
poverty rate for the American elderly is almost six times the
average of the other nations, while the U.S. poverty rate for
children is almost four times the average.

Table 5.1

Social Welfare Spending and Poverty in Six Western Nations

	Poverty rate[a]				Social Security and other transfers as a percentage of GDP[b]	Percentage of mother-only families with income below half of median income before transfers[c]	Present reduction in poverty by government benefits[c]
	Children	Working-age adults	Elderly	Overall			
Sweden (1987)	1.6	6.6	0.7	4.3	21.2	6.0	81.0
Germany (1984)	2.8	2.6	3.8	2.8	19.3	25.0	34.0
France (1984)	4.6	5.2	0.7	4.5	23.5	16.0	59.0
United Kingdom (1986)	7.4	5.3	1.0	5.2	13.7	18.0	75.0
Canada (1987)	9.3	7.0	2.2	7.0	12.8	45.0	19.0
United States (1986)	20.4	10.5	10.9	13.3	11.5	53.0	5.0

[a]Data from Smeeding (1992), reported in U.S. House (1993 [*Green Book*]): 1289.
[b]Data from Oxley and Martin (1991): 158–160.
[c]Data from Smeeding and Rainwater (1991).

Why are the American rates so high? Smeeding examined a number of potential explanations. One obvious explanation—that the American poor work less—proved to be untrue. The American poor seemed to work as hard as their European counterparts (Smeeding and Rainwater 1991). Another possibility is that perhaps America starts with a higher rate of prebenefit poverty. Interestingly, the opposite is true. In the year of comparison, Smeeding found that the pretax and transfer poverty rate in the United States was about 19.8 percent, compared to an average of 22.4 percent for the other nations. Thus, the European nations start with a higher poverty rate, but they spend more on assistance and their programs are designed to be more effective. Table 5.1 (column 5) shows that on average the European nations spend considerably more of their budgets on social welfare than does America. Those nations that spend the most tend to have the lowest rates of poverty. Well-targeted and more generous programs push between one-half and three-quarters of all the pretransfer poor over the poverty line. As we will detail below, these nations also tend to treat poor children as generously as they treat the aged. This, of course, is not true in America.

Table 5.1 (columns 6 and 7) also shows that mother-only families in Europe are in one sense an exception. Their pretransfer poverty rate is much lower than the rate for mother-only families in America. Using half of median family income as a poverty line, column 6 shows that over half of mother-only families in America are poor before receiving benefits, and, with the exception of Canada, this is much higher than the rate in the other countries. Sweden, France, and the United Kingdom have especially low rates of pretransfer poverty for mother-only families. Still, as with other demographic groups, European programs are quite effective in moving poor mother-only families out of poverty. In Sweden over 80 percent are removed from poverty, along with 75 percent in the United Kingdom and almost 60 percent in France. German and Canadian programs are less effective, but American programs are by far the least effective. Only 5 percent of American mother-only families receive enough benefits to move them above 50 percent of median income.

In the pages that follow we will examine the differences between European and American welfare programs, in terms of orientation, content, and goals, to determine if there are any lessons for American reform.

Some Limits of Comparative Analysis

Comparative analysis can provide interesting and even important insights into social policy, but conclusions must be tempered by caution (Mahler and Katz 1988). Several points should be kept in mind when comparing the successes of various countries in preventing, alleviating, or eradicating poverty or other social problems. First, social welfare programs are not the only means by which poverty can be prevented or alleviated. Countries with very healthy economies (especially very low rates of unemployment), egalitarian wage policies, and generous employee benefits may have less need for welfare programs.

Second, the size and diversity of the nation's population may also play an important role in determining how much poverty exists and how hard it is to alleviate. Large industrial nations with more complex economic and social problems and more diversity in race and ethnicity may well be faced with more complex problems. This is especially true when the progress of racial or ethnic groups has been held back by discrimination. The smaller industrial countries—Switzerland, Austria, Sweden, Finland, and Denmark, for example—are racially homogeneous, have no disadvantaged minorities, have quite egalitarian wage policies and excellent employee benefits, and have considerably fewer problems with illegal drugs and crime. These countries may have more success, in part, because they currently have less complex problems. This is not to suggest that these nations do not deserve credit for preventing many of the social problems that plague America, but prevention may be easier to accomplish in racially homogeneous nations of less than 10 million people.

Third, just because a particular program works well in one country does not mean that it could be adopted and would work as well in another. The national health insurance systems in most Western European countries, for example, were adopted before health care professionals became well organized and politically powerful. Since the end of World War II medical associations in the United States have been powerful enough to defeat proposals for fundamental reform of the health care system. In 1994 President Clinton launched a major effort to reform the health care system and extend coverage to the 40 million or more Americans without coverage. It took the well-organized and wealthy health care and insurance industries a relatively short period of time to defeat the president's proposals. This is not to say that America's health care system should not be reformed. But reform will have to deal with the reality of the health care power structure, and it is doubtful that in the next couple of decades America will have a national health care system like those found in Western Europe.

Fourth, there is a critical difference between dealing with poverty by maintaining families at an income level slightly above poverty and helping them obtain the skills, resources, or support required to compete in the work force. The United Kingdom, for example, often uses social welfare programs to maintain large numbers of families for long periods of time above poverty but considerably below median family-income levels. This approach keeps the families from suffering absolute deprivation, but it does not provide them with the type of education, job skills, or support they may need to earn a good living. Because the productive value of the recipients is lost, this type of welfare system creates a serious drag on the economy. The type of welfare program that best suits American philosophy is the type that empowers the poor to be independent, productive citizens. We will discuss examples below.

Fifth, despite the success of some nations in dealing with poverty, progress does not come easily, cheap, or without dissent. In recent years many of the nations of Scandinavia and Western

Europe have struggled with rates of unemployment that were often high by their historical standards, low birth rates, an aging population, high taxes, and, in some cases, sluggish productivity and growth (Bureau of the Census 1994a, 869). There has been considerable debate in many of these nations about whether welfare programs and generous wage and benefit policies are causing some of the problems. The nations vary in their attempts to cope with these problems, but none has abandoned a strong commitment to social welfare. Primarily the nations are trying to stimulate private pension programs to supplement public retirement programs, encouraging personal savings, modestly increasing the cost sharing for medical programs, extending the retirement age, and encouraging employment, especially for young adults. To promote childbearing and employment of both parents, family allowances, parental leaves, and child care benefits have been increased in many of the nations (Haanes-Olsen 1989; Lindbeck 1988).

Thus, while economic problems may result in social welfare programs' being judged more critically in many of these nations, the commitment to social welfare will remain high. Most Europeans fear that America's more austere approach produces high rates of crime, despair, drug use, and millions of dead-end jobs. Therefore, in the foreseeable future, European and Scandinavian social welfare programs and job benefits may be downsized somewhat and evaluated more carefully, but they will still be generous and expansive by American standards. And, as we have noted in Table 5.1, they will be effective in dealing with poverty.

The West European Approach

America's approach to social welfare policy is fundamentally different from that of most Western and Scandinavian countries (Furniss and Mitchell 1984). There are three major differences. First, most of the European and Scandinavian countries emphasize prevention of social problems, including poverty, by means of such policies as national health systems, extensive housing programs, and child or family allowances. Second, they have a belief that problems are best prevented if the most important programs are universal. Thus, these countries are less likely to use means tests for program eligibility (Wong, Garfinkel, and McLanahan 1993). Universal programs are not only more effective in preventing social ills, they generally enjoy broader public support and do not carry the social stigma often associated with means-tested welfare programs. Third, many of the countries try to ameliorate social problems by public intervention to keep the economy as healthy as possible, and employ programs to keep the public trained well enough to adapt to changes in the economy and international markets; and some distribute income more equitably by egalitarian wage policies.

Comparing American social welfare programs for low-income families with those of Western Europe reveals how significantly these differences manifest themselves in public policy. The United States is the only major Western industrial country (DeSario 1989; Kahn 1983; Kamerman 1980) that:

1. does not have a uniform cash-benefit program for poor families;
2. restricts cash-welfare benefits almost exclusively to single-parent families headed by women;
3. has designed its main cash-welfare program to discourage mothers from working;
4. has no statutory maternity benefits;
5. has no universal child-rearing benefits;
6. has no universal health care benefits (Kamerman 1984).

Some of the implications of these differences are fairly obvious. In the United States:

1. the primary emphasis is on dealing with families or individuals after, not before, they become poor or seriously ill;
2. assistance is designed primarily to deal with symptoms rather than causes, varies significantly by state, and is lim-

ited mostly to families headed by single women who often must remain single to receive essential assistance such as Medicaid;

3. little or nothing is done to move most welfare mothers into the job market, and in fact most are discouraged from seeking work by loss of cash and noncash benefits—such as Medicaid—and lack of supportive services (e.g., child care);

4. poor families normally can receive critical assistance (e.g., medical care) only if they stay on welfare;

5. most employed women cannot have a child without suffering serious wage loss, or even loss of their job.

The remainder of this chapter examines the major European programs and discusses the insights that might be applied in reforming American social welfare policies.

Child and Family Allowances

Every Western industrialized country except the United States provides a package of cash and in-kind programs to supplement the income of families with children (Kahn 1983; Kamerman 1980; Kamerman and Kahn 1981). Many countries call this set of programs a "family benefit" package. A central component is the child or family allowance, which can be found in sixty-seven countries (Haanes-Olsen 1989, 20; Kamerman 1984, 263). In most of them, including Canada, Belgium, and the Scandinavian countries, the allowances are universal and tax-free to all families, regardless of income or family structure. In some countries they are limited to families with two or more children, and sometimes they are means-tested. The allowances vary by the number of children in the family, and sometimes by the age of the children. France, for example, provides a larger supplement to families with young children. In all the major Western countries a special supplement is provided to single-parent families. None of the countries exclude families from these benefits because they are intact or because a parent is in the labor force.

The allowances were originally designed to increase the birth rate. Whether the grants ever had a significant impact on child-bearing is problematical, but they remain popular because they supplement the cost of raising children. By sharing the cost of child rearing, the society helps insure that the basic needs of children are met. The general belief is that children raised in a more financially sound environment will be healthier, better educated, and more productive members of society.

The size of the grants is generally small, but the evidence suggests that they are a significant aid to low-income—especially single-parent—families (Kamerman 1984, 263). This is especially true since the allowance is larger when there is a lone parent.

Housing Assistance and Allowances

Governments in Western Europe use a wide range of policies to subsidize the construction, purchase, and rental of quality housing. Their role in housing tends to be substantially greater than that of the U.S. government (Hallett 1988; Headey 1978; Leichter and Rodgers 1984; McGuire 1981). Many of the West European governments became involved in housing policy in an effort to overcome the destruction brought about by two world wars. Once involved, governments tended to stay involved. Both conservative and liberal political parties in Western Europe generally support an extensive role for the government in housing. The conservatives believe that government programs subsidize and stimulate the private housing market and the economy, while liberal parties add that decent housing for all should be a societal goal. Quality housing is a national resource because it is a durable good that also provides a healthier environment for families.

The governments of Western Europe use a wide range of housing policies, including public housing, saving bonuses to help families accumulate the down payment for a home, subsidies to builders of nonprofit housing cooperatives, assistance to home mortgage lenders, and housing allowances. Great Britain, for example, stresses public housing and housing allowances.

Even after a privatization movement, about 20 percent of all housing in Britain is publicly owned. A wide range of income groups live in this public housing, with rents reflecting the size and income of the family. Housing allowances are also used to assist families living in privately owned housing.

In Sweden some 45 percent of all housing was built with public funds, about 20 percent is owned by consumer cooperatives, and about 35 percent is privately owned. Regardless of sector, about 90 percent of all housing in Sweden is financed by the government. This policy lowers the costs of housing, making it generally more affordable. In addition, Sweden has a very generous housing allowance policy. About 50 percent of all families with children are eligible for a housing allowance.

The governments of France, West Germany, and the Netherlands all play a major role in housing. Like Sweden, these countries stimulate the housing market through quasi-public housing subsidized and financed by the government and run by quasi-public authorities. Public and quasi-public housing is not limited to low-income families in these countries; it is commonly occupied by middle-income families. This takes away any stigma on public housing and promotes a healthier housing environment. These countries also use housing allowances to assist families with limited incomes. West Germany and France provide larger grants to single-parent families; the Netherlands and Great Britain increase the grants to families whose rent is high in relationship to their income.

Single-parent families benefit greatly from the housing programs in all these countries. They are given preference in public or quasi-public housing and receive housing allowances. In some countries they receive a larger allowance to make up for the loss or lack of a second adult earner. In most of these countries the housing allowance, along with the family or child allowance, constitutes a significant income grant to single-parent families. As Kamerman (1984, 264–265) notes:

> If one adds the value of the housing allowance to the family allowance allotted a non–wage-earning mother the total accounts for al-

most half of her income in France, more than a third in Sweden, and more than a quarter in Germany and the United Kingdom; for the working mother, the transfers together constitute almost 40 percent of her income in France, more than 25 percent in Sweden, and close to that in the United Kingdom and Germany.

As Table 5.1 shows, one obvious result of the use of family and housing allowances is that single-parent and other low-income families are much less dependent upon means-tested welfare programs and they are much less likely to be poor.

Child Support

In recent years some countries have adopted a new approach to child support when one parent is absent. Austria, France, Denmark, and Sweden, among others, now use "advance maintenance payments" (Kahn 1988; Kamerman 1988; Kamerman and Kahn 1983). Under this program, all absent parents are taxed a certain proportion of their income each month. The proceeds are accumulated and used to provide a minimum monthly grant to all children with an absent parent. If the absent parent is unemployed or cannot be found or identified, the child or children still receive the minimum grant. An absent parent may also make additional contributions directly to the children.

The advance maintenance payments program enjoys growing popularity. One attraction of the policy is that it increases the chance that an absent parent will make regular payments. The program does so not by penalizing the parent, but by assessing the absent parent at a fair and regular rate. The burden on the absent parent is often reduced by the monthly tax, which keeps the parent from falling behind and then being obligated to pay a sizable amount to catch up. Additionally, children are not penalized if the absent parent cannot pay or cannot be located. Last, requiring absent parents to meet their child-care obligations reduces the likelihood that the custodial parent and children will need public assistance.

The advance maintenance approach would not work quite as well for poor Americans unless current U.S. policies were amended. The reason, as noted above, is that many of the European social welfare programs that support and assist low-income families are universal, with no means tests. By contrast, a single-parent family in the United States often becomes ineligible for health, housing, or nutritional assistance when income from a job or child support increases, even very modestly (Kamerman 1989). Some excellent research has shown that American states could amend their policies to make the policy quite viable (Garfinkel and Melli 1982; Garfinkel 1992).

Maternity Benefits

Most of the major Western European industrial countries have programs that protect the jobs and incomes of women for a period of time before and after childbirth (Kahn 1983; Kamerman 1980). Maternity leaves are generally covered by the country's social insurance program. This approach assures that a woman will receive the assistance regardless of the wealth of her employer. There is no means test for the program, benefits are in cash, and they are usually wage-related. In most cases a woman receives at least 90 percent of her normal wage up to some cutoff point. The leave lasts sixteen weeks in France and thirty-six weeks in Sweden, but most countries set the leave at twenty-four to twenty-six weeks, allowing for extensions for specified periods if the mother or child is ill (Kamerman and Kahn 1981, 71–73). Some countries allow a mother to extend the leave for a few weeks at her discretion, but at a reduced benefit level. Sweden allows the parents to decide, after the birth of the child, which of them will take the leave.

The social insurance programs also usually allow a mother to take a paid leave to care for a sick child at home. The mother usually receives 90 percent of her normal pay for a certain number of days. If the child's illness is extended, the mother is sometimes covered at the rate specified for personal illness under the social insurance program. Sweden allows either parent to take this leave.

Child Care

The issue of child care provides interesting insights into social welfare philosophy in the various nations (Kahn 1987). In many of the Western European countries, as in the United States, debates have taken place about the role that public authorities should play in child care. The family policies or family benefit packages that exist in Western Europe were built on the assumption that most mothers would remain at home until their children reached school age. As women have become more career-oriented and have formed a larger percentage of the work force, child care policy has had to be reexamined. Most European and Scandinavian countries have in recent years concluded that parents should be given the support they need to balance careers and parenthood (Kamerman 1991; Kamerman and Kahn 1988; Kamerman 1988; Kamerman and Kahn 1981; Rosengren 1973; Wagner and Wagner 1976; Young and Nelson 1973).

Three basic types of care are quite common: day care, usually for children up to age three; family day care arrangements, usually licensed and regulated; and preschool programs. Day care facilities are usually under the jurisdiction of health care authorities, as are family facilities that care for small numbers of children in a private home. Preschool programs are generally under the jurisdiction of the education ministry. Preschool programs emphasize cognitive development and preparation for school. Sweden and France have developed the most comprehensive programs.

In Sweden the day care centers are neighborhood-based and run by certified child care specialists. A board composed of center employees and parents sets broad policy and supervises the operation of the center. Fees reflect the salary of the parent, the number of children in the family, and how long the center cares for the child each day. Fees are kept modest to encourage center use, and they are lower for single-parent families. All of the centers have a developmental, as opposed to custodial, orientation. Each child receives educational, nutritional, and health care assistance. Some centers are open twenty-four hours a day for parents who work nights. Centers may share facilities with programs for retired citizens who can, if they wish, help out with the children.

France relies heavily on several types of day care and innovative preschool programs associated with the public schools (Kamerman 1991; Kamerman and Kahn 1988). The *écoles maternelles* are full-day preschool programs for children aged two to six. These programs stress cognitive and social development. Highly regarded, the *écoles maternelles'* sophisticated and comprehensive approach has yielded such positive results that other European nations are beginning to emulate them.

The major child care arrangements in these nations are substantially subsidized by the government. Costs are often quite high but the nations consider them excellent investments. The children receive quality care and educational benefits, and by keeping individual costs low, parents are encouraged to work rather than rely on social welfare. France and Sweden, particularly, provide an excellent lesson for other nations. Both have low rates of poverty among mother-only families, along with modest levels of public dependency. Excellent child care allows mothers in these countries to work rather than rely on public support (Garfinkel and McLanahan 1994, 215–217).

Interestingly, Japan, a nation that does not seem interested in encouraging mothers to work, has developed high-quality, affordable child care for working mothers. The centers are neighborhood-based and charge sliding-scale fees, with average costs in 1995 of about $200 a month. The poorest families receive the service free. Fees pay only about 20 percent of the total cost, leaving the government to pay the rest. The centers are for working women only, but the public has increasingly come to believe that children should have the experience of the nurseries. The result is that many Japanese mothers obtain work certificates even when they are not employed so their children can be admitted. The government seems to have concluded that the nurseries are important to the development of children. Thus a service that began as a way to help mostly lower-income women work has become a program mostly designed to benefit children. On that basis, the Japanese government has decided that it is a good investment (Kristof 1995, A4).

Health Care

Most advanced industrial countries in the West—except the United States—have a universal program of national health insurance or a national health service (Cairncross 1988; Leichter 1979; Navarro 1989; Roemer 1977; Simanis and Coleman 1980; Social Security Administration 1988b). These programs provide comprehensive health care to all citizens regardless of income, age, family structure, or employment status. Under these systems a family struggling on limited income cannot be made poorer by health care costs, nor does the family have to be officially designated as poor—and then stay poor—in order to receive health care assistance. Thus, the health care system is one method by which these countries prevent poverty and dependence.

All the countries at least attempt to place emphasis on preventive health care, which is considered less costly than an acute health care approach where people seek medical care only after they become ill. In a preventive system, emphasis is placed on health education and on such services as maternity care, prenatal and postnatal care, and basic medical screening for early detection of conditions that can cause serious illness. Most of the countries have networks of neighborhood centers that specialize in maternity and child health care. In France, mothers cannot receive their child or family allowance unless they schedule regular visits to these clinics for themselves and their children.

With the exception of Great Britain, all the major Western European industrial countries have national health insurance systems. Under these systems, most citizens become members of the national health insurance program through their employment. All employers are obligated to enroll their employees in an approved insurance plan that provides comprehensive health care coverage to the employee and any dependents. Both the employer and the employee pay a monthly fee, which provides most of the funding for the system. Any citizen who is unemployed or aged is enrolled in a health plan financed by the federal and/or local government.

Under national health insurance, participants select a doctor of their choice, who either treats them or, if necessary, refers them to a specialist. The doctors charge on a fee-for-service basis, but the government establishes the reimbursement rate. The patient may pay a small fee for services, especially if medical appliances or drugs are prescribed.

Germany was the first Western country to adopt a health insurance program, the Sickness Insurance Law of 1883 (Flora and Heidenheimer 1981; Sulzbach 1947). Originally the act covered industrial wage earners but not their families. In 1885 and 1886 the law was amended to bring some workers in commercial enterprises and farm work into the program. The program, financed by a tax on workers and their employers, provided medical care, cash sickness benefits, maternity benefits, and a cash grant for funeral expenses. The program was administered by sickness funds, a type of cooperative organization that had long existed in Germany. In 1885 there were almost 19,000 such funds.

During the first two decades of the twentieth century, the program changed in two major ways. Eligibility was extended to more workers and increasingly to their dependents, and benefits became more comprehensive. National standards for the sickness funds encouraged them to consolidate, which greatly reduced their numbers. Hundreds of amendments strengthened and expanded the program over the years. Currently almost all German citizens are covered by the program. Employees make monthly contributions, which are matched by employers. Some of the costs are financed out of general revenues. All citizens earning less than a regularly adjusted minimum income standard are required to participate in the program, and their dependents are automatically covered. Those earning above the standard may participate on a voluntary basis. Pensioners and citizens receiving unemployment compensation are covered by public programs.

Medical benefits under the German program are comprehensive, with modest cost sharing. In addition to comprehensive health care, the program provides sickness allowances, a household allowance so that families can hire assistance during an illness, a lump-sum maternity payment, and a cash grant to cover funeral expenses. Doctors are paid on a fee-for-service basis, with fee schedules determined by the federal government.

The national health insurance systems in other Western industrial countries work very much like the German system. These programs provide high-quality comprehensive coverage for all citizens, a goal that has eluded the American health care system.

Great Britain is the exception among European nations. It employs a national health service to meet the needs of its citizens. Great Britain passed a national insurance plan in 1911. The initial plan covered workers, but not their dependents. The 1911 act was designed to supplement and, in part, take the place of worker organizations known as friendly societies, cooperative organizations that pooled fees to provide workers with cash benefits during illness, medical care by a contracted physician, and an allowance to cover funeral expenses.

The 1911 act covered only workers earning less than an established income standard. The program was financed by worker and employer contributions and general tax revenues. Covered workers received physician care (but not hospitalization) and sickness, disability, and maternity benefits. The friendly societies were pacified by being allowed to administer all but the medical benefits. By the 1940s only about 40 percent of the population was covered under the act (Leichter 1979, 167).

To overcome many of the inadequacies of this approach, the National Health Service Act was passed in 1948. Under this act, the government assumed responsibility for financing hospital and clinic construction and for training and hiring medical personnel. Unlike a national health insurance system, the government became the owner of the country's hospitals and clinics and the employer of most doctors and other medical personnel. Some 85 percent of the cost of the program is financed by the central and local governments. Employers and employees pay modest insurance premiums that finance another 10 percent of costs. Cost-sharing and user fees provide the other 5 percent of financing.

Every British citizen is covered under the act, and the benefits are comprehensive. Citizens receive routine medical care by registering with a physician of their choice. General practitioners receive a fee for each patient registered with them. As a cost-cutting incentive, group practitioners are allowed to have more patients than solo practitioners. Hospital and surgical care is provided by physicians who are salaried employees of publicly owned hospitals. Patients pay a small fee for dental and ophthalmic services and for prescriptions. There are normally no fees associated with routine medical and hospital services.

The British Health Service has been plagued by a very weak national economy, preventing the nation from increasing funding to upgrade medical services. Still, the British National Health Service, like the health insurance programs found in the other Western nations, provides comprehensive health care to all citizens, regardless of their income.

Interestingly, the comprehensive health systems of these countries are more economically efficient than the American health care system. In 1991, for example, health expenses in the United States equaled 13.4 percent of gross domestic product. In the same year health expenditures were 8.4 percent of GDP in Germany, 9.1 in France, 6.2 in Great Britain, 8.6 in Sweden, 7.6 in Belgium, 8.6 in Austria, and 10 in Canada (Bureau of the Census 1994a, 859).

Market Strategies

Some of the Western industrial countries have expressly opted to use economic strategies, sometimes combined with social welfare programs, to reduce poverty and the long-term need for means-tested assistance. One of the most common strategies is egalitarian wage policies, used mostly by the Scandinavian nations. In these countries the differences between the wages of low- and high-skill workers are moderated so that all employed workers can afford to live decently. In these nations income and lifestyle differences are much less dramatic than in most other capitalist nations. Additionally, to keep unemployment rates as low as possible, many nations use a combination of strategies including manipulation of interest rates, public investments in the private sector, and government job training, relocation, and employment programs (Furniss and Tilton 1979, 134–138). By contrast, American administrations have often used economic policies to increase the unemployment rate as a method of reducing or controlling the rate of inflation.

Keeping unemployment low and wages more egalitarian is often part of a more complex economic strategy. Sweden, for example, has made economic efficiency a key element in its market approach. The Swedes believe that their industry must be modern and highly productive in order to remain competitive in international markets. This means that industry must constantly innovate to promote productivity, and that weak, inefficient businesses must be weeded out. The maintenance of obsolete or inefficient jobs is not allowed because this would reduce efficiency. Workers and unions do not have to struggle to protect obsolete jobs, for workers whose jobs are abolished are assured of other, equally good positions. If the worker needs retraining or relocation, he or she receives this help with pay during the transition period. Thus, low unemployment is part of a larger economic strategy designed to keep the economy healthy, competitive, and prosperous. Sweden recognizes that only this type of economy can produce the surpluses needed to provide a wide range of supportive human services.

In recent years, all Western nations have had to deal with the fact that they increasingly live in a global rather than a local or national economy. Strategies that once worked have had to be altered to deal with the reality of competing in this expanding global market. Some of the nations of Western Europe that were long successful in keeping unemployment low and wages high have struggled to adapt to a rapidly changing economic environment. Still, as noted above, the commitment to using social welfare programs to respond to and participate competitively in the world economy remains high. Basic economic data seem to support this commitment. While social welfare expenditures are on average about twice the level found in the United States (see Table 5.1 [p. 109]), the economies of Western Europe and Scandinavia have enjoyed an annual growth rate over the last couple of decades equal to the growth of the American economy (Oxley and Martin 1991, 159).

Summary and Conclusions

The social welfare systems of other major Western industrial societies differ from the American system in several important respects. First, most of these countries provide a broader core of universal, non-means-tested assistance programs to all citizens. The most obvious example is the package of programs provided to all citizens through the health care system. Second, the countries have programs specifically designed to assist families with children. These programs are either universal or provided to almost all middle- and low-income families. All the countries make this package available to lone-parent families, with many giving such families a larger supplement. Third, none of the countries deny assistance to intact families or require a lone parent to stay unemployed, single, or poor to qualify for, or remain qualified for, critical assistance such as housing or health care. Fourth, the cash-benefit programs are uniform for all poor families, regardless of family structure (Kamerman and Kahn 1988).

Because of the benefits that citizens receive from programs such as national health insurance, family allowances, varied housing programs, and maternity leaves, fewer low-income families need income-tested cash-welfare assistance. The universal and other broadly provided assistance programs thus increase the security, independence, and presumably the dignity of low-income families, allowing them more options for work, training, or education. France has specifically altered and expanded its

social welfare package in recent years to give greater assistance
to lone-parent families and to allow low-income women a choice
of staying home with their children or entering the labor force.
Sweden has designed its system to facilitate management of si-
multaneous work and parenting roles by both parents.

This review suggests that for several reasons the social welfare
programs of Western Europe are more efficaciously designed than
the U.S. programs. First, they better meet many of the basic, critical
needs of citizens. This is especially true of health care, housing, and
maternity leave programs. The universal financing of such programs allows all citizens to enjoy these benefits regardless of the
wealth of their employer. Second, they do not require a parent to be
single or remain single or unemployed in order to receive needed
assistance. These negative incentives are built into the American
system. Third, they provide a uniform level of benefits to all poor
families, including intact or single-parent families that fall on hard
times. There are lessons here that could inform alterations in the
American approach to social welfare.

Some Western European programs are particularly imagina-
tive and provide cues about how American programs could be
improved. Most obvious is the advance maintenance payments
program now in effect in a number of countries. Sweden's uni-
versally financed maternity leave, which can be used by either
parent, and the broadly available housing allowances found in
Germany, France, and Sweden are other good examples. The
well-financed child care and preschool systems in France and
Sweden significantly lower dependence in those nations by making it possible for parents to participate in the work force while
better preparing children for school.

Last, the market strategies of some of these countries yield a
critical insight. The health of a country's economy is the key
predictor of the poverty rate (Tobin 1994). Public policies designed to keep unemployment low, real wages competitive, productivity high, and industries competitive, and to support, retrain,
and relocate those out of the job market are critical means by
which a nation can limit poverty.

Chapter 6

Reforming the American Welfare System

Establishing, updating, or revising welfare programs has never been easy in the United States. As noted in chapter 4, it took the crisis of the Great Depression and the turmoil of the 1960s to produce the patchwork system of programs that we currently refer to as the American welfare system. Richard Nixon tried diligently to reform the welfare system, hoping to substitute a version of the negative income tax for most of the extant programs. Under a negative income tax, a family's or individual's income is compared to a predetermined poverty standard. If a family's income is below the standard, the family has a "negative income" and the government will transfer income to the family. Families below the standard with earnings receive more assistance than those without earnings. Nixon's plan was twice passed by the House, but it expired in the Senate.

Although President Nixon's proposal finally failed, for a time it promoted a consensus about the most plausible approach to welfare reform. Gerald Ford made a modest effort to recoup Nixon's momentum on the issue by offering another reform package based on the negative income tax. Ford abandoned the effort when the economy turned increasingly sour. Jimmy Carter hoped that welfare reform would be a major accomplishment of his administration. He proposed a system based on a negative income tax for those able to work, and a guaranteed income for those who were unemployable. President Carter's plan also foundered in Congress.

The defeat of Carter's plan cast a pall over reform for most of a decade. The concepts on which that plan was based had been debated during three administrations, and it seemed clear that Congress was unlikely to accept reform based on substantial use of the negative income tax plan. The consensus upon which debate centered during three administrations had clearly dissolved (Ellwood 1989, 269).

A New Consensus—Supported Work

President Ronald Reagan's idea of reform consisted of three principles: (1) compulsory work programs for the poor; (2) reducing, consolidating, or abolishing as many welfare programs as possible; and (3) convincing the states to assume a larger share of the costs and administrative burdens of those programs that survived. Equally important, Reagan convinced Congress to cut federal taxes while substantially increasing spending for defense. Reagan's theory was that the tax cuts would stimulate the economy and produce more, not less, tax revenue. Time proved Reagan wrong. The result of Reagan's failed policies was the largest deficits in the nation's history. The huge new national debt made it even less likely that Congress would entertain welfare reforms that significantly raised federal outlays, even temporarily (Tobin 1994). Additionally, in the early and mid-1980s there was no generalized crisis of the magnitude that had spawned programs in the 1930s, 1940s, 1960s, or early 1970s to lend urgency to welfare reform. Poverty increased quite dramatically during the Reagan years, but Reagan was successful in dismissing this as a temporary aberration of his economic policies.

While Reagan's convictions never changed, by the end of his

presidency a new consensus on welfare reform was developing in Congress and at the state level. The new consensus is that poverty alleviation can best be achieved by programs that train or educate welfare mothers for employment and then provide them with short-term support to help them become established in the work force. This approach is usually known as supported work and is often based on a mutual obligation contract between a welfare recipient and the state. This approach is substantially different from programs that simply require some welfare recipients to work in return for benefits. These new programs emphasize education and training and are backed by programs such as child care and medical benefits to help the family head stay in the work force. This new approach was the foundation of the Family Support Act passed in 1988.

The Family Support Act of 1988

In some ways the Family Support Act (FSA) was not a major departure from past welfare reform approaches. There have long been work programs associated with AFDC. But in the past, few welfare recipients were actually placed in job search, education, or job training programs, and recipients who left AFDC for work received little or no support. The FSA was somewhat more comprehensive, but it was not designed to impact a very large percentage of AFDC recipients initially. The FSA was very modestly financed, and it was phased in over a five-year period. The importance of the FSA was its philosophical foundation in training and supported work and its assumption that both parents should be responsible for the welfare of their children.

The goal of the FSA was to reduce considerably the time that families remain dependent on AFDC by providing recipients with the education, confidence, and job skills required by the labor force. To make employment a viable option, the bill financed child and health care for enrolled mothers and extended these support services to the family heads for a limited period while they became settled in the job market. The bill also emphasized improving child support from absent parents. The major provisions of the bill were in five titles.

Title I. Child Support and Paternity

Starting in November 1990, all states were required to provide wage withholding of child support in all cases in which the custodial parent receives public assistance or in those cases in which the custodial parent has asked for assistance in collecting support. In 1994 states were required to institute wage withholding of child support for almost all support orders. More uniform guidelines for all child support awards were required by the bill and these guidelines are to be reviewed on a regular basis.

By fiscal 1992 all states faced penalties if they failed to establish paternity in a certain proportion of all cases of children born out of wedlock and receiving benefits. To help states locate missing parents, the bill provides access to both IRS and unemployment compensation data. Procedures were established to collect child support from noncustodial parents residing in a different state.

Title II. Job Opportunities and
Basic Skills Training Program (JOBS)

All states were required to establish a JOBS program. All single parents with children over three (or at state option, over one) are required to participate, unless they are ill, incapacitated, or have some other valid reason for nonparticipation. States were given a great deal of discretion in designing the training programs, but they have to be approved by the Department of Health and Human Services at least every two years. All states were required to have the JOBS program in place by October 1990 and statewide by October 1992.

The FSA requires the state agency in charge of AFDC to assess the needs and skills of all AFDC heads. From this consultation an employability plan for each recipient is developed, specifying the activities the head will undertake and the supportive services the participant will receive. State programs must include education, job training, job preparedness training, and job placement. Postsecondary education and other approved employment activities may also be offered. Parents under age twenty without a high school diploma are required to participate in an educational program leading to graduation. Some states have also been allowed to set up programs to provide education, job training, and placement to noncustodial parents.

In an effort to reduce long-term welfare dependency, the bill requires the states to spend at least 55 percent of all JOBS funds on (1) families that have received assistance for more than thirty-six months during the preceding five years; (2) families in which the head is under age twenty-four and has not completed high school; and (3) families that will lose benefits within two years because of the age of their children.

Title III. Supportive Services

The states are required to provide child care to participants engaged in education, employment, or job training. To help recipients stay in the work force and leave the welfare roles, the state can assist in child care for up to one year. The cost of the care to the parent is based on a sliding scale. Families leaving the AFDC ranks because of employment are eligible for Medicaid coverage for up to one year.

Title IV. AFDC Amendments

The bill requires all the states to establish an AFDC-UP (unemployed parent) program to cover two-parent families with an unemployed head. Until the FSA, only about half the states allowed two-parent families to receive AFDC benefits. States new to the program may at their option limit benefits to a minimum of six months a year. However, Medicaid benefits would have to be ongoing.

The amount of money that an AFDC family can earn without reducing benefits was raised to $90 a month from $75. The amount that a parent can spend on child care was raised from $160 a month to $175 (or $200 if the child is under age two). Expenditures for child care are not counted as income in calculating AFDC benefits. States may require single parents who are minors to reside with a parent or guardian.

Title V. Demonstration Projects

The bill funds a rather wide range of innovative demonstration projects at the state level to determine how well various experimental programs alleviate problems or promote certain desirable outcomes. For example, $6 million over a three-year period was allocated to encourage innovative training and education programs for poor children. The sum of $3 million was authorized to fund programs to train poor family heads to be child care providers. Eight million dollars was provided to establish programs to improve noncustodial parents' access to their children. Other programs provide counseling for high-risk teenagers and incentives to businesses to create jobs for AFDC recipients.

The Impact of the Act

It is too early to evaluate the Family Support Act. Perhaps its most important impact has been philosophical. Most conservatives and liberals seem to agree, at least in principle, that AFDC recipients should receive education, training, and supportive services to help them become independent of welfare. There is also broad support for holding both parents responsible for the sustenance of their children. Establishment of paternity and support from the noncustodial parent have both increased as a result of the act (U.S. House 1994, 500–501). States have been slow to establish JOBS programs, with many asking for delays. In 1994 only about 13 percent of all AFDC heads were receiving JOBS training. Of those JOBS programs in place, quality evaluations of their impact have yet to be carried out. Based on experience with job training and job search programs since the early 1970s, most experts expect JOBS programs to have a modest but positive impact on welfare participants (Blank 1994, 188–191). This will be discussed in more detail below.

One of the most important consequences of the FSA has been a great many very innovative welfare reform experiments at the state level. The FSA allows the states to petition the Department of Health and Human Services for waivers that provide them with the flexibility to be creative in the design of their welfare programs. The waivers permit states to treat welfare recipients within the state differently as long as they are participating in an approved experiment. The state must also agree to pay for any additional costs associated with the implementation and evaluation of such experiments. By late 1995, about half of the states had either obtained or applied for waivers, allowing them to substantially renovate their welfare systems.

The Clinton Administration Plan

President Clinton had considerable experience with welfare as governor of Arkansas and included welfare reform in his presidential platform. Once elected, President Clinton put together teams of experts to design a plan that would "end welfare as we know it." The Clinton administration plan is based on the continued use of entitlement programs to ensure that all the eligible poor are given assistance. It rests on four principals:

I. Make work pay. Provide incentives that make it more profitable for families to work than to receive welfare. This goal rests primarily on expanded benefits under the Earned Income Tax Credit (EITC), a program for working parents with dependent children, and on expanded child care and Medicaid coverage for those leaving or avoiding welfare by entering the work force.

II. Improve child support enforcement. Improve the system for identifying and forcing absent parents (usually fathers) to support their children. Mandatory support payments will be collected through wage withholding. Women who fail to cooperate in identifying the father of their children would receive reduced benefits. All unwed teen mothers under eighteen would be required to live with a parent or guardian to be eligible for AFDC. Funds would be allocated to help states establish anti-pregnancy programs for teenagers based on counseling, moral suasion, and incentives.

III. Help AFDC heads obtain jobs. Expand and improve the job training, education, and support programs authorized by the Family Support Act of 1988. Almost $10 billion would be allocated to job training and child care subsidies to move AFDC mothers into the work force and help them stay employed.

IV. Set time limits on cash benefits. Recipients who were born after 1972 and are healthy and able to work will be expected to accept the combination of education, training, or placement help required to allow them to leave the rolls, often within two years. This provision has been popularly termed "two years and out." If these mothers cannot find employment in the private sector, a low-wage public sector job will be provided or the government will subsidize the cost of their employment in the private sector. Transitional child care and Medicaid coverage will be provided to help the mothers become established in the world of work. The goal of this provision is rather modest: to move 400,000 mothers into training programs by the year 2000.

President Clinton summarized his proposal in a speech to the National Governor's Association in early 1995: "Anyone who can work should do so. Welfare reform should include time limits. Anyone who brings a child into this world ought to be prepared to take financial responsibility for that child's future. Teen pregnancy and out-of-wedlock childbearing are important problems that must be addressed through comprehensive welfare reform."

The GOP Plan

In 1995 the Republican Party had a majority in both houses of Congress. One goal of the Republican majority was a thorough overhaul of the nation's welfare system. Throughout 1995 the

House and Senate struggled to agree on a welfare reform bill, with the House passing its first version of a reform package in March 1995. In September 1995 the Senate passed a more moderate reform plan. In late October 1995 the welfare reform plan was sent to a conference committee to try to iron out differences between the House and Senate versions. By early December 1995 some of the conference committee decisions had become public. The bill being debated by the conference committee differs from the Clinton approach in some important ways. The major provisions of the bill being considered by the conference committee late in 1995 are:

I. Cap welfare spending. The Clinton plan would continue to treat major welfare programs as entitlements, meaning that all persons who qualify for benefits under a program would be served. The Republican plan eliminates entitlements and places a yearly cap on most federal welfare spending.

II. Turn welfare programs over to the states. Many current welfare programs would be consolidated into block grants to the states. Each state would receive a lump sum payment each year under each of the block grants and be given considerable discretion in designing its own welfare programs. The House and Senate bills differ over whether states should be required to continue their welfare spending at current levels. The conference committee compromise would require the states to continue spending for cash welfare programs at the 75 percent level. The major block grants are:

A. Temporary Assistance to Needy Families Block Grant. The House bill consolidates AFDC and three related programs into a yearly $15.4 billion block grant to be divided among the states. Federal costs would remain constant at $15.4 billion until 2000. The Senate version funds this block grant at $16.8 billion a year. Both the House and Senate bills would give the states discretion to transfer some of these funds to other poverty programs such as nutrition or child care.

B. Child Protection Block Grant. The House bill consolidates twenty-three federal programs such as foster care, adoption assistance, and child abuse prevention and treatment into a $4.4 billion block grant in 1996, rising yearly to $5.6 billion in fiscal 2000. The Senate bill leaves these programs intact. The conference committee accepts the Senate position.

C. Child Care and Development Block Grant. The House version folds nine existing federal child care programs for low-income families into a $1.94 billion block grant. The Senate version sets aside $1 billion annually for child care plus $3 billion over five years in matching grants to the states.

D. Family Nutrition Block Grant. The House bill replaces the Women, Infants and Children (WIC) program, the Summer Food Program, the Homeless Children Nutrition Program, and parts of the Child and Adult Care Food Program with a $4.6 billion block grant in fiscal 1996, rising yearly to $5.3 billion in fiscal 2000. The Senate bill does not include WIC in this grant.

E. School-Based Nutrition Block Grant. The House bill replaces the school lunch and breakfast programs as well as the school-based summer food program, Child and Adult Care Food Program, special milk program, and the commodities portion of the school meal program with a $6.7 billion grant in fiscal 1996, rising yearly to $7.8 billion in fiscal 2000. The Senate bill leaves these programs at the federal level but reduces expenditures for each of them.

III. Allocate block grant funds. Under both the House and Senate bills, the $15.4 billion block grant would be distributed among the states using the same formula used to distribute AFDC in 1994 or the average of fiscal 1992–94, whichever is higher. States would also receive financial incentives for reducing out-of-wedlock births. Beginning in 1997, $100 million annually would be divided among those states with growing populations. Additionally, states with unemployment rates of at least 6.5 percent could borrow from a $1 billion rainy-day fund. Distribution of funds among the states for the other major block grants would basically reflect each state's current funding for the programs included in the grant.

IV. Require time-limited assistance. Under both the House and Senate bills, states would be required to cut off cash benefits to any family that has received assistance for a lifetime limit of five years, or to any adult who refuses to cooperate in establishing paternity or who fails to assist a state child support enforcement agency. If a recipient has received a year of training, benefits could be ended after two years. Any adult recipient who has received two years of welfare would be required to engage in work activity, including education and job training. States would be required to enroll half of all caseload family heads in work or training programs by 2001 or suffer a 5 percent reduction in funding. The goal would be to require 1.5 million welfare family heads to find employment by the year 2001. Recipients who become ineligible for cash assistance could still qualify for noncash assistance such as Medicaid and food stamps. The conference committee bill would allow states to exempt up to 15 percent of their caseload from the five-year limit.

V. Deny or reduce cash assistance to some families. The House bill stipulates that unwed teen mothers under eighteen would be ineligible for cash assistance, except in cases of rape or incest. States could extend the ban to all unwed mothers under age twenty-one. Children born to families on welfare would also be denied cash assistance. The savings could be used to fund orphanages, adoption services, and homes for unwed mothers. States could issue vouchers to teen mothers and to women who have children while on welfare, to be used to purchase baby supplies. Cash benefits for a family would be reduced by 15 percent, up to $50 a month, in cases in which paternity has not been established.

The original Senate bill leaves it to state discretion as to whether teen mothers and children born to welfare mothers could receive cash benefits. The conference bill accepts the House version but stipulates that a state could overturn this provision by majority vote of the state legislature.

VI. Eliminate most aid to legal immigrants. Under the House bill, immigrants legally admitted to the United States would no longer be entitled to Supplemental Security Income (SSI), cash welfare, social services block grant funds, Medicaid, and food stamps until they became citizens. The only exceptions would be refugees, permanent residents over age seventy-five who have lived in the United States for at least five years, legal immigrants who served in the U.S. military, and, in some cases, immigrants who have been residents for five or more years. The Senate version grants aid from some programs only to legal immigrants who have resided in the United States for at least five years, and grants other assistance only to those who become citizens. Both the House and Senate bills extend the financial responsibility of immigrant sponsors, sometimes until the immigrant becomes a U.S. citizen or pays Social Security taxes for ten years.

VII. Change Food Stamp rules. Under the House bill, the Food Stamp program would not be rolled into a block grant but would become a capped entitlement. Annual expenditures would be capped but everyone qualified by need would receive assistance. If demand was high, each recipient would receive less. All able-bodied food stamp recipients would be required to obtain employment within ninety days or enroll in job training or a government-sponsored work program. The Senate version does not cap Food Stamp expenditures, but it does reduce benefit levels. The conference committee bill would allow states the option of accepting block grants to operate Food Stamp and school lunch programs of their own design without federal rules.

VIII. Tighten eligibility for SSI. Under both the House and Senate bills, adults suffering from drug addiction or alcoholism would no longer be eligible for Supplemental Security Income (SSI). The definition of a disabled child would also be changed. Under current law a child is disabled if mental, physical, and social functioning is substantially less than that of children of the same age. Under the new law a child is disabled if he or she has a medically verified physical or mental impairment expected to cause death or last more than twelve months. The conference committee bill provides that less-disabled children would receive 75 percent of the benefits paid to the most-disabled children.

IX. Enforce child support orders. Both the House and Senate bills would establish new state and federal registries to help enforce child support orders. States would be required to establish a central-case registry to monitor all child support orders. They would also be required to establish a worker registry to which employers would send the name, Social Security number, and address of all new hires. The states would be required to put Social Security numbers on most licenses and to suspend licenses of parents who fall behind in child support payments. Federal registries would be established to track absent parents nationwide.

President Clinton's Reaction

In December 1995 the Republican majority was still expressing confidence that it would be able to produce a compromise bill from conference, pass it in both houses, and send it to the president for signature by the end of the year. However, President Clinton announced in early December that the bill being written by Congress was unacceptable to him and that he would veto it.

President Clinton's objections to the Republican bill include the following:

I. Capped spending. The president wants to continue to fund welfare programs as entitlements.

II. Financial commitments of states. Clinton wants the states to continue to spend at current levels or very close to current levels on poverty alleviation.

III. Lack of emphasis on job training and child care. President Clinton favors time limits for cash welfare and strong work requirements, but he wants a guaranteed job, in the public sector if necessary, to be available for recipients who leave the rolls. Clinton also wants the states to expand child care and health services for welfare recipients who leave the rolls to accept a job.

IV. Cutbacks in nutrition programs and the EITC. President Clinton fears that the Republican reform proposals would result in increased hunger and malnutrition among the poor, especially poor children. Additionally, the President fears that Republican cutbacks in the EITC (considered below) would make it more difficult for the poor to escape poverty through employment.

While President Clinton may not accept the GOP welfare reform bill, at least not unless it is revised to deal with most of his objections, the Clinton reform approach is a substantial break with the past. Both the Clinton and GOP plans show impatience and lack of faith with the way welfare has functioned in America over the last three decades. Both plans are designed to reduce the amount of time that families remain on welfare, substantially reducing the number of long-term welfare recipients. The Clinton plan is basically an extension of the Family Support Act of 1988. It attempts to control costs by making both parents accept responsibility for the financial support of their children, by shortening welfare spells through time limits, and by helping welfare 'recipients obtain the skills, experience, and support required to become established in the job market. Unlike the GOP plan, the Clinton plan guarantees public sector or subsidized jobs to AFDC heads who cannot find regular private sector employment when they leave welfare.

The GOP plan, on the other hand, controls costs more directly by ending or capping entitlements and by imposing stricter eligibility requirements and time limits on welfare recipients. The most radical feature of the GOP plan is that it turns primary responsibility for welfare over to the states and greatly increases their discretion in designing and implementing welfare programs. The GOP plan places less emphasis on educating, training, assisting, or supporting adults who move into the job market and does not guarantee public sector or subsidized jobs to those who leave the rolls. The bill requires the states to enroll 50 percent of their caseload in work activities by 2001, although a 1995 study by the Congressional Budget Office concluded that forty-four states could not meet this goal (*Congressional Quarterly Weekly Report* 1995, 2004). Welfare families would be dropped from the rolls after five years regardless of whether they had obtained training or other job-related assistance. The evidence suggests that most families would leave the rolls without ever having received any education, training, or counseling.

The GOP plan also bases much of its proposed savings on greatly restricting assistance to legal immigrants. While legal immigrants as a category are not citizens and so cannot vote, they are obligated to pay taxes and they cannot be deported. If federal benefits to legal immigrants are greatly constrained, the states may come under considerable pressure to pick up the costs for immigrants who become dependent. This would probably lead to more pressure on the federal government to restrict immigration.

Like the Clinton plan, the GOP legislation expects both parents to accept financial responsibility for their children and significantly strengthens enforcement. The Clinton plan seeks to reduce births to unwed teens through counseling and incentives, while the GOP plan cuts off all cash aid. The GOP proposal is strict but is softened by allowing the states to provide vouchers to be used for baby supplies and by allowing state legislatures to override the ban on cash aid.

The GOP proposal to cap the cost of welfare programs may not disappear even if President Clinton vetoes the welfare bill. Entitlements are a major reason for the federal government's ever-increasing budget and deficits. As Congress struggles to reduce expenditures and deficits, welfare and other entitlements are very likely to be cut back and/or capped in the future. The problem with a cap is that unless states are diligent in helping poor families escape poverty and innovative in preventing poverty, they might run out of designated funds and then be unable to assist many of their poor or end up spending more state dollars on the poor. A serious economic downturn might also significantly increase the number of poor, leaving the states without the required resources or forcing them to borrow from the federal government.

The strict term limits contained in both the Clinton and GOP plans may have a positive impact on many family heads. Knowing that there is a real limit to assistance, many family heads may take more seriously the obligation to obtain the education, training, and support required to become established in the job market. Unfortunately, term limits and caps will also bring hardship to many families. Some heads of welfare families, perhaps as many as a quarter, will—because of addiction or other problems—be unable or unwilling to become established in the work force. Other adults may find job opportunities limited. Children of these adults will be the major victims. States may be given the authority or flexibility to exempt some families. States will also have the authority to place more children in institutions or foster or adoptive homes.

In late July of 1995 President Clinton altered his plan in two ways. First, he issued an executive order prohibiting Food Stamp benefits from increasing when a family is thrown off AFDC because the family head refuses to work. Since Food Stamp benefits are based on family income, a family thrown off AFDC has less income and therefore is qualified for more food stamps. The president's order changed this rule.

Second, the president ordered the Department of Health and Human Services to give fast-track approval to state welfare reform plans featuring any one or a combination of five policies. Rather than the usual 120 days, the president ordered review and approval within 30 days if the plans involved: (1) strong work requirements for welfare family heads backed up by adequate child care; (2) strict time limits backed by public sector jobs for those adults who cannot find employment in the private sector; (3) programs that require teen mothers to live at home and stay in school as a condition of assistance; (4) improved child support enforcement; and (5) conversion of welfare and Food Stamp benefits to cash subsidies to employers who hire welfare recipients.

State Welfare Reform under Clinton

President Clinton's new initiatives have nurtured the welfare reform that has been taking place at the state level since the passage of the Family Support Act in 1988. By the end of 1995 twenty-four states had received approval or had applied for waivers allowing them to substantially reform their welfare systems. Some of the state plans that have been approved and put into operation at the state level are more radical than Clinton's basic plan. Still, the Clinton administration has approved them, allowing welfare reform and innovation to take place in many states.

The new state plans stress limiting the amount of time that families remain on the welfare rolls. They have names that reflect a determination to help welfare recipients obtain the skills and support they need to move as rapidly as possible into the work force. A few examples include:

- Massachusetts: Transitional Assistance Program;
- Georgia: Personal Accountability and Responsibility Project;
- Florida: Family Transition Program;
- Utah: Single Parent Employment Project;
- Virginia: Independence Program;
- Wisconsin: Work, Not Welfare Program;
- Colorado: Personal Responsibility and Employment Program;
- New Jersey: Family Development Program;
- Mississippi: Work First.

All of the new state programs have the goal of limiting the amount of time that recipients may remain on the welfare rolls, often to two years or less for any single spell, with a five-year lifetime limit. Recipients are expected to accept responsibility for themselves and their children, and to obtain those skills necessary to find employment. Some of the states require recipients to enter into mutual obligation contracts that spell out the responsibilities of the state and the client. Most of the states help recipients find jobs, with job search assistance being more prevalent than job training. Child care assistance and Medicaid coverage are generally extended during the first year of employment; some states provide assistance for much longer periods.

Many states have strengthened the mandatory work requirements for welfare heads, sometimes by cashing out benefits and allowing employed heads to keep more of their earnings from employment before payments are reduced. Other states have cashed out benefits to subsidize jobs for welfare heads or mandated that welfare heads accept community service jobs. Several of the states are raising recipient asset limits to enable recipients to afford more reliable transportation and even build up some modest savings. Some of the states have adopted the Family Cap, which denies additional assistance to a mother who gives birth to additional children while on assistance. Most require teenagers to live with a parent or guardian in return for assistance. Most of the states provide serious penalties, including loss of all assistance, to recipients who fail to cooperate with training, education, and placement or paternity programs.

Some states have adopted Learnfare programs, which use either reductions or enhancements in benefits to encourage recipient children or teenage single parents to stay in school or earn a GED (Long, Wood, and Koop 1994; Martinson and Friedlander 1994). Bridefare or Wedfare programs have been adopted by some states. These programs offer financial incentives to welfare mothers who marry and leave the rolls for specified periods. Some states have implemented Healthfare programs, which require welfare mothers to have their children immunized as a condition of continuing support (Wiseman 1993).

A few state programs demonstrate how these various reform options are being combined. Early in 1995 the state of Massachusetts combined three options to create one of the most restrictive welfare programs in the nation. Under this program, about one-third of all welfare recipients classified as able-bodied will be expected to find work within sixty days or accept public service jobs. Women on assistance will not receive additional benefits for children born while they are on welfare. Benefits will end once a recipient has received twenty-four months of coverage. Exceptions to the two-year limit can be granted in special cases of hardship by the state welfare commissioner. Teen parents will be allowed to receive benefits only if they stay in school and live with a parent or guardian. Massachusetts officials do not expect these new policies to have much immediate impact on the state's welfare costs. While the number of recipients will decrease, the state will spend considerable more money on child care to enable parents to work. Over time, however, the state expects to reduce welfare costs significantly.

Michigan now requires able-bodied recipients to work twenty hours a week in return for assistance. Women must return to work within six weeks of having a child. By the end of 1995 almost 200,000 welfare heads in Michigan were working in return for benefits. Mississippi is cashing out benefits to fund private sector jobs, limiting assistance to two years, and has adopted the Family Cap. New Jersey has adopted the Family Cap, placed time limits on welfare assistance, and requires most recipients to work. Medicaid coverage is extended to those who leave the rolls to work. Florida limits assistance to twenty-four months in any sixty-month period, provides child care for up to twenty-four months, and has adopted both Workfare and Learnfare programs.

The waiver system requires that the states carefully evaluate the impact of these experimental programs. While quality evaluations are not yet available, by the end of 1996 the impact of these reform measures should be increasingly clear.

The Clinton, GOP, and many of the new state plans rest on a recently expanded Earned Income Tax Credit and, in varying degrees, a better funded and managed JOBS program. Both are examined in more depth below.

The Earned Income Tax Credit

Fundamental to Clinton's welfare plan is that those who work should not be poor. One of the primary ways that Clinton proposes to lift workers above the poverty line is by a recently expanded Earned Income Tax Credit (EITC). The GOP has long supported the EITC, which was added to the Internal Revenue Code in 1975. The EITC was originally designed to provide an annual earning supplement to parents who maintain a household for a child and have modest earnings. In 1994 the EITC was extended to nonelderly adults without children who earn low wages (Leonard and Greenstein 1993). The EITC tax credit is refundable. If the parent or worker does not owe any taxes or has a tax obligation lower than the credit, he or she receives a direct payment from the Internal Revenue Service. This program gives low-income workers a "work bonus" or incentive to work, and compensates for the regressive impact of the Social Security tax.

The value of the EITC as an antipoverty strategy has become increasingly apparent over the years. The EITC has been popular with Congress because it rewards the work ethic while subsidizing low-wage jobs. The 1993 Omnibus Budget Reconciliation Act significantly expanded EITC benefits through 1998, when the annual cost will rise to $24.5 billion. The earning supplement provided to low-wage workers is substantial. In 1996, for example, a family with two children will receive a refundable tax credit of 40 percent of the first $8,425 in earnings, a maximum of $3,370. Families with two children with earnings above $8,425 but below the cutoff point of $27,000 will also receive refundable tax credits. Haveman and Scholz (1994, 14) have calculated that in 1996 the EITC will raise the value of a minimum-wage job to a family with two children from $4.25 an hour to $5.95. Scholz (1994) estimates that more than 6 million workers with incomes below the poverty level will receive supplements under the program in 1996. About 1 million families will be lifted over the poverty line by the credit.

The EITC, especially in its newly expanded form, does play a major role in making work pay for low-wage families. Since the credit is not considered salary, it does not reduce the benefits that a family might receive under other programs such as AFDC or Medicaid. Still, there are problems. First, since the EITC is a tax credit, families who receive a cash bonus must wait until the end of a tax year, file an income tax return, and then wait for a lump-sum refund check. The family would be better off if an income estimation process could be used that would even out payments over the year. The advantages of this approach are as obvious as the perils and complexities. Second, the provisions of the EITC are fairly complex. Low-income workers, and even case workers, may not be able to estimate the value of the credit, significantly reducing the incentive value of the program. Third, even in its expanded form, millions of low-wage working families with children will be left below the poverty level. Fourth, while the EITC improves the wages of low-income workers, it does not play a role in increasing the number of jobs for inexperienced and low-skill workers. Fifth, as part of its budget reduction plan in 1995, the GOP eliminated coverage for adults without children and proposed major funding reductions. It is not clear whether President Clinton will accept these changes.

Haveman and Scholz (1994) suggest that the EITC could be supplemented in a couple of ways. First, they recommend that Congress reconsider a policy initiative known as the New Jobs Tax Credit (NJTC), which was in effect in 1977–78. The NJTC was designed to encourage employers to add entry-level jobs. It did so by providing a subsidy equal to 50 percent of the first $6,000 in wages paid to the fifty employees hired by a firm in excess of 102 percent of its previous year's work force. Evaluations found that the program was successful in creating new jobs for low-skill workers at a very reasonable public cost. Two studies concluded that up to 30 percent of all new jobs in the studied industries resulted from the program (Bishop and Haveman 1979; Perloff and Wachter 1979).

Another option suggested by Haveman and Scholz (1994) would combine with the EITC and NJTC to significantly increase the value of work to low-wage employees. This plan involves the government's directly subsidizing employees who earn less than a targeted wage, say $8 an hour. If a worker earned less than $8 an hour, the government could pay some share of the difference, say 50 percent. Thus, an employee earning $6 an hour would receive a $1-an-hour subsidy, while accumulating the benefits of the EITC. The advantages of this policy are obvious. The employee makes a better income and receives the benefits in each paycheck received over the course of the year. The problem that would have to be resolved is how to make certain that the employer does not set wages at unreasonably low levels in hopes of letting the government pay more of his or her labor costs. This would clearly require government review of employer wage rates, which could be difficult and expensive, perhaps even quite intrusive.

The combined impact of the NJTC, the EITC, and some type of wage subsidy program would be a powerful stimulus to the job market and would certainly make work pay. As welfare reform moves more toward helping recipients, absent parents, and young men become established in the work force, more emphasis may be placed on stimulating the job market and making certain that there is a clear advantage to working. While the Haveman and Scholz proposals may need some fine tuning, it is clear that subsidizing jobs and wages is less expensive, more effective, and probably more popular than creating jobs in the public sector.

Job Training Programs

The FSA, Clinton's welfare reform plan, and to a lesser extent the GOP plan are all based on job training programs for welfare family adults. Since World War II the federal government has financed a large number of major job training programs, for both welfare and nonwelfare families. The Job Opportunities and Basic Skills (JOBS) training program established by the FSA grew out of the experiences of federal job training programs, especially the Work Incentive Program (WIN), which it replaced (GAO 1994d; GAO 1994e).

The Clinton welfare reform plan is based on an expansion of the JOBS program, which is still in its infancy at the state level. Under the GOP plan the states would also rely on JOBS to move welfare heads off the rolls. The design and objectives of JOBS are generally well thought of, but the program currently covers only a small proportion of poor family heads and it is too early to accurately measure its impact. The basic goal of JOBS is to provide the training and support required by AFDC parents to enable them to be successful in the job market. Since the FSA obligated the states to set up new programs with rather modest funding, required participation rates are modest. Starting in 1990 at 7 percent of nonexempt recipients in each state, the standard increased to 15 percent in fiscal year 1994 and 20 percent in 1995. Exempt recipients are: (1) those who are ill, incapacitated, or aged; (2) anyone who is caring for an ill or incapacitated person in the caregiver's home; (3) anyone caring for a child three or younger, or, at state option, younger than one; (4) those employed more than thirty hours per week; (5) children under sixteen attending school full-time; (6) women in at least the second trimester of pregnancy; and (7) those residing in an area without a program. Exempt recipients are free to volunteer for the program. Those exempted constitute a sizable percentage of all AFDC heads.

Requirements for AFDC-UP families are more stringent. At least one parent in these two-parent families is expected to work at least sixteen hours per week. The percentage of AFDC-UP families the state is required to have meet this standard increases yearly from 40 percent in 1994 to 75 percent in 1997. The states can substitute education programs for work to meet the standard.

The basic services offered by the state JOBS programs are: (1) educational services designed to help recipients earn a high school degree or equivalent, obtain basic literacy, or become proficient in English; (2) job readiness programs; (3) job skills training; (4) job development and placement; and (5) supportive services. States must also offer two of the following activities: (1) on-the-job training; (2) group and individual job search; (3) work supplementation programs; (4) community work experience (CWEP) or another type of work experience program. States may, at their discretion, also offer postsecondary education.

Under JOBS, an AFDC applicant may be required to engage in a supervised job search for up to eight weeks and all AFDC recipients may be required to engage in a job search for as many as eight weeks each year. If an AFDC recipient receives any type of education or job training services, the state may require additional periods of supervised job search. AFDC heads may also be placed in community work experience programs as long as they receive valuable work experience or training that may lead to regular employment. The number of hours a recipient may be required to work is calculated by dividing his or her monthly AFDC benefits by the federal minimum wage, or by the state minimum wage if that is higher. Every six months the recipient must be reevaluated to update his or her employability plan.

One of the most interesting options under JOBS is work supplementation. Under this option the state may use a welfare recipient's monthly allocation to fund or subsidize a job for that recipient. The job becomes a substitute for a welfare check. The job can be in the public or private sector. To make this option more valuable for recipients, the state may allow the employed recipient to keep the first $30 plus one-third of all other earned income without a reduction in benefits. The state is required to extend Medicaid coverage to recipients who participate in the program. The federal government limits its financial contribution to its share of the cost of AFDC for the family for nine months. After that point, the state would have to pay the full cost.

AFDC recipients involved in any JOBS education or employment program are entitled to child care. Child care must also be provided on a transitional basis to AFDC heads who leave the program because they have found employment or have increased their hours of employment. Transitional child care assistance may be provided for up to one year.

The Impact of Work Programs

The JOBS program has not been in place long enough to have been carefully evaluated. Other relatively recent work-welfare programs run by the states have been scrupulously evaluated. The Manpower Demonstration Research Corporation (MDRC) is a research institute that has helped many states design and evaluate work and training programs for welfare heads. MDRC's findings about the impact of state-run work-welfare programs most likely provide insight into the role that the JOBS program can be expected to play in alleviating poverty (Gueron and Pauly 1991).

While MDRC has found that the impact of employment programs varies somewhat by state, several findings are consistent. First, AFDC parents who receive education and job training are more likely to leave welfare, obtain employment, and earn more while employed than AFDC recipients who have not received this assistance. The earning gains are, however, rather modest; usually less than $800 annually. Most of the income gain results from working more, not from higher wages. Second, job search programs, even rather modest ones, seem to work. AFDC mothers in these programs are considerably more likely to find employment. Third, the programs pay for themselves through a combination of higher wages and less dependence on welfare programs (Gueron and Pauly 1991; Gueron 1987).

The impact of work and education programs on welfare recipients is fairly consistent with those found for job programs for nonwelfare recipients. Adult women who received job training, education, and on-the-job training under the Comprehensive Employment and Training Act (CETA) improved their earning ability, but the dollar gains were between $1,270 and $2,100 annually (U.S. Congressional Budget Office and NCEP 1982, 19). Recent evaluations of the Job Training Partnership Act (JTPA) programs show that adult participants gained, on average, less than $750 a year in wages, but this exceeded program costs (Bloom et al. 1993, 4).

The evidence from these job training programs indicates that they do yield positive gains, pay for themselves, and reduce dependence on welfare programs. Still, there is no evidence to indicate that they play a major role in reducing poverty, at least not in the short run. It is unlikely that large numbers of poor mothers will be lifted above poverty, or at least much above it, by JOBS programs. In fact, the best evidence suggests that most AFDC mothers are likely to need continuing support services and supplements, even if they are employed.

Of course, training programs for welfare recipients may become more sophisticated with experience, and the government's commitment may increase. At least one respected expert believes there is considerable room for improvement. Heclo (1994, 407) characterizes the more recent efforts of the federal government and most of the states as ". . . a sorry chronicle of half-hearted, poorly administered, and politically orphaned gestures. Isolated from the unmet needs of the larger work force and without a strong administrative capacity for manpower policy in Washington, work and training programs for welfare recipients have languished in their own virtual policy ghetto."

Some job training programs work better than others, and the qualities of the better programs are being identified. Mead (1986, 152) describes successful WIN programs as positive environments in which both the administrators and the trainees are committed to self-sufficiency and both are expected to perform. The staff believes that all trainees can and should be employed, and that jobs are available if everyone works to provide trainees with the right skills and attitude. Relying heavily on job searches worked, as did getting participants into jobs quickly. Agencies were also more successful if they maintained close relationships with area businesses. Behn (1991) analyzed welfare work training programs in Massachusetts and concluded that management quality was extremely important. Successful programs had staffs that set high goals, believed in the mission, expected hard work and imagination from both staff and trainees, and provided the resources required to get the job done. Built into the program was a quality monitoring system that tracked the performance of both the staff and the trainees with the goal of identifying problems or areas for improvement.

Employment and job training programs will be central to the welfare reform programs proposed by Congress in 1995. The evidence suggests that they will have a positive impact on recipients, especially if they are designed and managed well. Still, a significant percentage of welfare mothers who graduate from these programs and become employed are likely to be economically vulnerable and in continued need of supportive public services. The EITC will assist many of them, as will the Food Stamp program. But many may also require assistance in obtaining health care and quality child care. It is not clear that this help will be available.

What's Missing in These Plans?

As intense as the public debate about welfare reform is, the plans being debated by Congress are deficient in some important ways. Comprehensive reform would require more attention to out-of-wedlock births, child care, preschool and education programs for low-income children, and better child support. Each issue is examined below.

Dealing with Out-of-Wedlock Births

One of the most serious obstacles to significantly reducing poverty in America is the high rate of out-of-wedlock births. As noted in chapter 3, almost 30 percent of all births in recent years have been to never-married women, including some 68 percent of all births to black women. Never-married women who gave birth as teens constitute an ever-increasing proportion of all AFDC recipients, and they tend to stay on the rolls for extended periods of time. Even the best-designed JOBS programs will not significantly reduce the overall rate of poverty until fewer children are born to parents who are financially, educationally, and sometimes emotionally unable to support them. To significantly reduce poverty, in other words, the sources and causes of poverty must be addressed.

How do we reduce the number of out-of-wedlock births, especially to high-risk teens? Comparative data show that American teenagers of all races have a much higher rate of abortion and pregnancy than do teenagers in other Western industrial nations. This is true despite the fact that the level of sexual activity of American teenagers is about the same as that of teenagers in other Western countries (Weatherley 1988, 114). Weatherley

(1988) points out that other Western nations manifest more liberal attitudes toward sex, provide more comprehensive sex education, and provide easier access to contraceptives.

Studies from the United States show that reducing out-of-wedlock births is not easy. Especially where high-risk teens are concerned, only very comprehensive programs have proven effective. Programs that consist of two-hour sessions once a week for six to eight weeks for teens and usually one or more of their parents and emphasize communication, high self-esteem, assertiveness, peer-pressure resistance, and abstinence have shown no positive effect on high-risk teens (Christopher and Roosa 1990; Roosa and Christopher 1990).

More comprehensive programs that are taught over longer periods—one or more semesters—by teachers who have received special training, and which rely on classroom presentations, discussion groups, peer counseling, and individual counseling, *have* shown positive results (Zabin et al. 1986; Zabin et al. 1988; Vincent et al. 1987). These programs stress abstinence but provide contraceptives to teens who are sexually active or who choose to engage in sexual activity. Many of these programs rely on after-school clinics that provide counseling, medical examinations, and contraceptives. These programs work best when they are backed up by community-wide courses for parents, the local clergy, and the media. The more community support they receive, the more effective they are. Effectiveness also goes up when the programs are part of a more comprehensive effort to prevent school failure and teen dropout. These programs are not without controversy or expense, but given the centrality of out-of-wedlock births to the whole problem of American poverty and the cost of welfare, a solution to this problem is critical.

As noted above, the welfare plans being debated by Congress place some emphasis on reducing out-of-wedlock births by placing obligations, penalties, and restrictions on the parents. Both the Democratic and Republican plans emphasize making both parents, married or not, financially support their children. While many low-income men will not be able to contribute significantly to the financial needs of their children, an understanding that bringing a child into the world involves long-term obligations may force men at all income levels to take this act more seriously. The result might be some reduction in out-of-wedlock births. Both parties also agree that unmarried teenage mothers should not be allowed to receive any type of welfare benefits unless they live with a parent or guardian. This policy might discourage additional births and it might improve the environment of the child.

Also as noted above, several states have decided that teens should not receive cash assistance, nor should AFDC mothers receive additional assistance for children born while they are on welfare. The GOP plan would make this national policy. As detailed in chapter 4, there is no evidence that teens or other women have babies to obtain or increase welfare benefits. Denying benefits would financially punish mothers and might play some role, probably modest, in discouraging out-of-wedlock births. There is reasonable fear, however, that such policies might increase abortion rates and that more children might be abandoned, neglected, or abused.

The House Republicans briefly endorsed orphanages as an alternative to financially supporting unwed teen mothers. This proposal provoked an interesting national debate. At first critics dismissed the idea as Dickensian and extremely expensive. The Child Welfare League of America pointed out that residential care in an orphanage costs about $36,500 per year per child (*Congressional Quarterly Weekly Report* 1995, 160). The media rushed to do stories on existing orphanages and found, possibly to their surprise, most of them excellent. Some school administrators and welfare workers pointed out that many of the children they deal with would be much better off in a safe and well-run group facility than in the crime-, alcohol-, and drug-infested environments in which they live. Still, there was broad agreement that orphanages are a very expensive option and that taking children away from their parent(s) is a drastic measure.

The Clinton welfare plan proposes to lead a national campaign against teen pregnancy, but the specifics are unclear. Basically, Clinton seems to be suggesting a counseling and public relations campaign against teen pregnancy, run primarily by the public schools. Clinton's proposal seems to go beyond current programs by publicly campaigning against out-of-wedlock pregnancies. It is not clear how effective this would be, but it would probably reflect the public mood. In 1992 President Bush's vice president, Dan Quayle, was initially jeered for criticizing a popular television program for glamorizing an out-of-wedlock birth. But the public rallied around Quayle. President Clinton eventually endorsed Quayle's position on family values. The media has debated the topic rather intensely over the last couple of years. The growing consensus seems to be that out-of-wedlock teen births must be seriously reduced. In his 1995 State of the Union address, President Clinton stated that significantly reducing births to unwed teens would be a major goal of his administration. The public seems to agree and may be willing to support increasingly strong measures to achieve that goal. If public relations, counseling, and incentives do not work, the public may become increasingly willing to support fund cutoffs and other harsh measures.

A more productive short-term approach would be to extend the use of the effective school-based programs described above. Long-term, the best solution is quality education. One of the clearest findings in the research literature is that when females are given a quality education they delay childbirth and have fewer children (Kakwani and Subbarao, 1994, 86–94). It is optimism about the future that prompts young women to make more rational choices about when to have children and how to balance childbearing and career goals. Unfortunately, millions of American teens do not feel very optimistic about their futures, in part because their educational experiences have not been positive. Many of them entered the public schools poorly prepared and receive little educational guidance or support from their parents, most of whom are themselves poorly educated. The type of quality preschool and child care programs discussed below might play a positive role in helping students enter the public schools better prepared to take advantage of educational opportunities. In the long run, this might turn out to be the best antidote to out-of-wedlock births.

Child Care, Preschool Programs, and Education

Chapter 5 examined social welfare plans in other Western nations. An interesting finding was that nations such as France, Sweden, and Japan have creatively used publicly financed child care to promote parental employment, adult education, and reductions in welfare dependence while providing valuable services to children. The programs are expensive, but considered worthwhile because they accomplish important social goals.

America's approach to child care is considerably different. As noted in chapter 4, in recent years the federal government has significantly expanded funding for child care where the parent is enrolled in a JOBS program, where the working parent needs child care help to avoid becoming eligible for AFDC, and as transitional assistance while a former AFDC recipient becomes established in the job market. These programs are recent in origin and enroll a modest number of children. These services would be expanded under the Clinton welfare proposal and would be more discretionary under the GOP plan. The federal government funds child care for low-income, impoverished, and special-needs children under several dozen other programs, but again the total number of children served is rather modest (U.S. House 1994 [*Green Book*], 544).

Other than welfare families, the federal government has never really considered playing a major role in the provision of child care. The primary method by which the government assists working parents is with a nonrefundable tax credit for child care expenses. For one child the credit applies to the first $2,400 of costs, and for two or more children it is based on expenses up to $4,800. The value of the credit decreases with income. Families with a gross income above $28,000 are allowed a credit equal to 20 percent of qualified expenses. The maximum value of the credit is $720 for one child and $1,440 for two or more children. Most families using the tax credit have incomes over $25,000. Low-income families receive little benefit from the credit because they generally do not have enough federal tax liability to use this option. While the tax credit is beneficial to working parents, it is too modest to have a significant impact on the provision or quality of child care.

Congress has in recent years debated whether to significantly expand the federal role in child care. The debate has been fueled by the rapid growth in the demand for child care, the knowledge that current child care arrangements are often not optimal situations for children or parents, and an increasing awareness that early training can greatly influence children's development and learning ability. Demand is fueled by the fact that the majority of women with children are now employed. Most are not employed full-time year-round, but the increase in employed mothers has been so substantial that the demand for child care has doubled and tripled over the last two decades. In 1960 about 30 percent of all women with children were employed. By 1993 employment had risen to almost 67 percent. The most significant increase has been among married women with children under six. In 1960 only about 19 percent were employed. In 1993 almost 60 percent were employed (U.S. House 1994 [*Green Book*], 534). Among all women with children, the least likely to be employed are never-married women with children under six. But even among this group of mothers, 47 percent were working in 1993 (U.S. House 1994 [*Green Book*], 534). Kamerman and Kahn (1987) have estimated that by the year 2000 some 75 percent of all mothers will be employed outside the home.

A majority of children under five in child care are in care outside their homes, with the largest percentage being kept either by relatives (16%) or nonrelatives (21%). Only 27 percent are in some type of organized child care facility. Of this group only about 2 percent are in kindergarten or grade school, while 8 percent are in a nursery school or preschool program. The great majority of children under five, therefore, are not in programs that emphasize the cognitive development of the child.

Unfortunately, careful evaluations of both family day care arrangements and child care centers find most of them to be of very poor quality. A 1995 study of four hundred child care centers in four states concluded that the vast majority of children were receiving mediocre care (Helburn et al. 1995). Most of the centers met health and safety standards and only some 12 percent of the centers were found to be unsafe and/or unsanitary. The major deficiency of the centers was that the intellectual and emotional needs of the children were neglected. Only one in seven of the centers provided a positive environment that focused on the developmental needs of the children.

The researchers found that the high-quality centers had the highest staff–child ratios, paid their staff members better, and required them to have more training. The quality programs tended to have extra funding from state or federal agencies, to be associated with universities, or to be funded and managed by employers. The quality centers spent about 10 percent more than those centers providing mediocre services. To improve quality, Helburn et al. recommended that: (1) child care providers have child development certificates; (2) states enhance their standards for child providers; (3) both the states and the federal government increase their financial support for child care; and (4) parents be given some assistance in understanding how to evaluate the quality of care their children are receiving.

Efforts to expand quality child care would also have to deal with three other problems: inadequate supply, lack of knowledge about options, and cost barriers. In some parts of the country, day care centers have six- to twelve-month waiting lists. Also, low-income mothers often are uninformed about publicly or privately financed child care options. Cost is a major problem for many families. Studies indicate that care for one child under five averaged about $63 per week in 1991 (U.S. House 1994 [*Green Book*], 541). This would be a yearly cost of over $3,000. Obviously, costs in this range are prohibitive for many families, especially those headed by a lone parent.

Young and Zigler (1986) have recommended three methods by which the federal government could play a role in expanding and improving the quality of day care. First, they propose establishment of a national day care clearinghouse within the federal bureaucracy. The clearinghouse would provide public officials, parents, and care providers with the latest and best information available on the characteristics, impact, and operation of quality day care. Second, they recommend developing a model for day care programs based on Head Start, which emphasizes an educational partnership between parents and providers. A central component of these model programs would be a parental right to unlimited access to their child's program, and a responsibility on the part of the provider to furnish parents with periodic progress reports (Young and Zigler 1986, 53).

A third suggestion is that public schools provide child care for three- to twelve-year-olds. The schools would provide care before and after school during the school year and full-time during vacations and summer months. This, of course, is the model used in France, Sweden, and Japan. The authors recommend that the public schools provide a family support system for first-time parents, information and referral services, and support services for private day care homes where most children under three are served.

This type of policy approach would significantly enhance the state's role in the provision of quality preschool and school-based educational programs to the nation's youth. The need to provide children with better preschool and after-school educational care is widely recognized. The better educated and nurtured children are, the more likely they will be successful in school and in the work force. Children in poor families and disadvantaged neighborhoods are particularly in need of early intervention. In addition to basic educational needs, they frequently need health and nutrition assistance. They also need guidance in areas fundamental to their futures, such as how to develop good study habits, how to deal with peer pressure, how to avoid drugs and crime, and how to delay sexual activity and pregnancy. They frequently need help in developing and maintaining self-esteem.

In many impoverished neighborhoods, the public schools might well be designed to provide at-risk and abused children not only with early educational assistance but also with a safe haven from the mean streets and conflicted environments in which they live.

Providing students of all ages with a quality education is the surest way to reduce poverty. As Figure 6.1 shows, there is a very high correlation between level of educational attainment and poverty. Adults twenty-five and older with less than a high school degree suffer a poverty rate of over 26 percent. The rate is even higher for blacks and Hispanics who do not graduate from high school. Adults who have graduated from high school have a much lower rate of poverty, although the rate remains high for blacks and Hispanics. Obtaining some college experience again lowers poverty rates substantially, while adults with a college degree are much less likely to be poor. When college graduates do suffer a spell of poverty, it tends to be short unless serious illness or disability is involved.

Single mothers also benefit greatly from education. As Figure 6.2 shows, over half of all single mothers without a high school degree are poor, regardless of race. A high school degree significantly reduces their rate of poverty, but the rate remains quite high. College experience short of a degree again lowers the rate of poverty for single mothers, but leaves rates at unacceptable levels. A college degree greatly lowers the rate of poverty for single mothers, regardless of race.

Given all the debate about how to eradicate poverty in America, education is a somewhat neglected topic. Far too little emphasis has been placed on reducing poverty by adopting a national goal of providing all children with a quality education. This goal would require that childhood education begin earlier and that performance standards for teachers, students, and schools be adopted and achieved. Much of the cost of public schools is already being paid. Studies reviewed in chapter 4 also show that well-designed education programs produce very positive, long-term results.

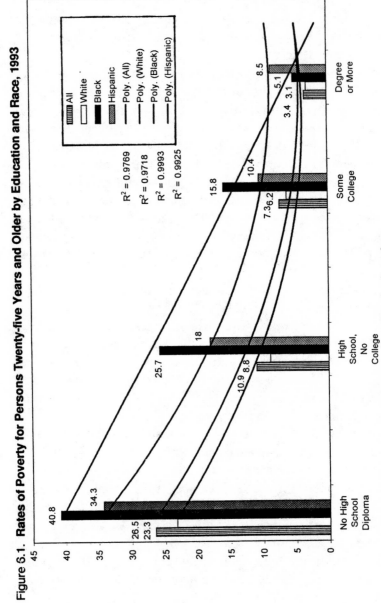

Figure 5.1. **Rates of Poverty for Persons Twenty-five Years and Older by Education and Race, 1993**

Source: Data are from unpublished 1993 census. Computations by the author.

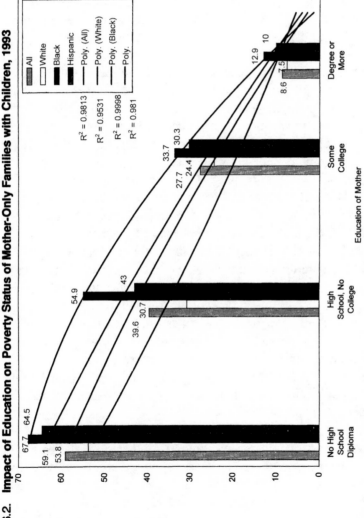

Figure 6.2. **Impact of Education on Poverty Status of Mother-Only Families with Children, 1993**

Source: Data are from unpublished 1993 census. Computations by the author.

Child Support Assurance

A great deal of progress has been made in increasing child support from absent parents (Garfinkel, Melli, and Robertson 1994). The FSA built on a number of laws passed since the mid-1970s and greatly strengthened child support enforcement. The reforms of 1995 will also strengthen child support. But, as noted in chapter 3, many children still receive no support from their absent parent and millions of other children receive inadequate support. Garfinkel and McLanahan (1994, 219) have estimated that if federal and state laws can continue to be refined until the child support system works perfectly, about one-quarter of the poverty gap for mother-only families will be eliminated. This would be an improvement, but children will still need public support.

Garfinkel (1992) has suggested an interesting alternative. The Child Support Assurance System (CSAS) would require all parents not residing with their children to pay a monthly tax toward their support. This tax would be deducted from their pay check, much like Social Security. The tax would vary according to the number of children and the income of the nonresident parent. For example, the tax on the first $60,000 in earnings might be 17 percent for one child, 25 percent for two children, increasing to a maximum of 33 percent for six or more children. All funds would be pooled and all children with an absent parent would receive a monthly benefit equal to the tax or a minimum, whichever is higher. If a child's absent parent could not be located, the child would still receive assistance each month, equal to the minimum benefit set by law.

The advantage of this plan is obvious. All children with an absent parent would receive support—either from the parent or from federal revenues. The least support a child could receive would be the minimum set by law. Children of a poor, unemployed, or unidentified parent would still receive assistance. Demonstration projects are currently being conducted in Wisconsin and New York to determine whether the plan would lower the poverty and dependency rates and produce a net saving. Several years into the project, the outcomes have been quite positive (Garfinkel 1992).

A simulation of the implications of implementing this program nationwide produced very interesting insights. The researchers generated three models based on varying levels of success in collecting from absent parents and various levels of guaranteed benefits. They found that at 70 percent, 80 percent, or 100 percent effectiveness, the program would reduce the poverty gap for poor families between 38 and 53 percent, and that AFDC caseloads would decrease by 48 to 64 percent. At 100 percent collection effectiveness, the program would generally produce a saving, with the cost rising above current levels as collection effectiveness falls and benefit levels increase (Garfinkel, McLanahan, and Wong 1988, 80).

These findings strongly suggest the value of improving child support across the nation. Resistance to this approach is based on fear that a guaranteed income for children with an absent parent would encourage more families of this type. It is difficult to project whether this would be true. If the CSAS were a part of a more comprehensive package designed to reduce births to unwed teens and identify absent parents, the advantages might very well outweigh the disadvantages.

A simulation recently conducted by Kim, Garfinkel, and Meyer (1994) suggests not only the value of an assured child support program, but the importance of using a combination of well-coordinated programs to combat poverty. The authors simulated the impact of the government's offering to all families with children (poor and nonpoor) a refundable tax credit, national health insurance, and an assured child support benefit. The authors simulated the effects of each program operating on its own, and of all three acting in concert, on poverty, AFDC rolls, and the incomes of poverty families. The authors found that the cumulative impact of the three programs was greater than the sum of impacts produced by each program alone. With all three programs in force, the authors found that the poverty rate would drop by 43 percent and the AFDC rolls by 22 percent, AFDC recipients would work more hours, and the annual income of poor families would increase by $2,500.

Conclusions

The data presented in chapters 1 and 2 show the changes in poverty demographics that have resulted in single women and their dependent children becoming a majority of all the poor in America. The data also show that the fastest-growing type of family in America is that headed by a single woman. In the last twenty years, mother-only families have more than doubled. In 1960 only one in ten families with children was headed by a single women. In 1993 almost one in four families with children was headed by a single women. Similarly, in 1960 only 8 percent of all children lived in a family headed by a single woman. By 1993 almost one in four children lived only with their mother. Ominously, mother-only families with children are more than five times as likely to be poor as married-couple families with children. As an increasing percentage of all families with children become mother-only, poverty among children has increased to tragic proportions. In 1993 almost one in four children lived in poverty, the highest poverty rate among children since 1964. Children are now the poorest major age group in America.

The analysis in chapter 2 revealed that the rate of poverty for mother-only families has always been high, and that the rate has not changed dramatically over the last two decades. What has changed is the number of mother-only families. As this type of family has increased as a proportion of all families, the high rate of poverty for such families has greatly expanded the number of poor, especially the number of poor children.

A number of factors have contributed to the increase in female-headed families, but the most important are rising rates of divorce, separation, and single parenting. All the evidence indicates that, at least over the next decade, the number and proportion of all families headed by single women will continue to grow. The implication is obvious: without significant change, poverty will remain high and children will be the major victims.

What type of changes will it take to reverse this pattern? The required changes can be discussed in four categories, but they are interconnected and complimentary. First, it should be understood that poverty can never be solved if the primary policy focus is on the poor. The policy emphasis must be shifted from dealing with symptoms to treating the source of the problem. If we are to end poverty, the problems that handicap Americans by making them economically marginal and vulnerable to poverty must be addressed. To greatly reduce the poverty pipeline, that seemingly endless flow of people vulnerable to poverty, America must substantially decrease the number of out-of-wedlock births, especially to teens, and do a substantially better job of educating its citizens to enable them to compete successfully in an increasingly sophisticated world economic market. The statistics on the growing major impact of families formed by unmarried teens on the welfare system document how important it is to target this problem. Additionally, as noted in chapter 3, millions of Americans continue to enter adulthood each year without a decent education or marketable skills in an economy that increasingly requires better-educated workers. The result is not only high rates of unemployment and subemployment, especially for many young minority males, but salaries for less-skilled workers and families of all races that have failed to keep pace with inflation. Thus, more people who work full-time struggle for economic solvency, contributing to increased family instability and less viability in relationships.

Second, the welfare system must be designed to work better. America's complicated and expensive welfare system has placed too little emphasis on preventing poverty and on the timely resolution of those conditions or personal problems that make people poor. The Family Support Act of 1988 established a model of providing welfare heads with the education, job training, assistance, and support that they required to become established in the job market. Most of the states are attempting in varying degrees to base their welfare programs on that model, and national welfare reform will most likely push them even more in that direction. The welfare reforms being debated in Congress and the innovations being approved by the Clinton administration will also enhance state flexibility and creativity, while requiring the states to deal with individual families within a fixed time period. It is predictable that there will be failures and required adjustments. But if the emphasis is placed on mutual obligations between recipients and the state, with programs designed to ameliorate barriers to independence, American welfare programs will hopefully be grounded on a model better designed to move people from poverty to independence.

Third, America's social policy needs to be designed to support the changing role of women and the changing nature of families. In most American families today, including those with children, both the husband and the wife are employed. And, of course, there are millions of single parents in the work force. This is a demographic change that is apparent across the Western industrial nations. Yet, other nations have accepted and supported the change better than America. High-quality child care, preschool programs, and better-designed public schools not only accommodate the work needs of families, they provide critical, even sophisticated, assistance to children.

Fourth, to expand opportunities for all Americans, the government needs to strike a better balance between the goals of inflation control and economic growth. The Federal Reserve goal of 2.5 percent annual growth is deliberately conservative, weighted on the side of inflation management as opposed to economic growth. Tobin (1994, 164–167) and other economists have pointed out that as all the world's major economies become more deregulated and globalized, prices and labor costs are disciplined while productivity increases. The result is that economies can grow faster without courting inflation. Higher growth is in turn associated with full employment and higher rates of productivity. When businesses grow they hire more employees, pay them better, train them better, and provide them with more opportunities.

In 1994, despite conservative federal policies, the economy

grew 4.1 percent and still produced almost no inflation. With superior growth, economic opportunities expanded and the poverty count dropped from 39.3 million in 1993 to 38.1 million by the end of 1994. Minorities, single mothers, and young adults made the largest economic gains. The evidence has always shown that a healthy, growing economy is critical to reducing poverty. Growth rates for the American economy must be brought up to par with changes in the world economy.

These reforms individually, and particularly in combination, would play a major role in reducing poverty in America. The cost would not be modest, but in the long run these expenditures would be cost-effective investments in building a healthier and more prosperous nation for all Americans.

Bibliography

Acs, G. 1993. "The Impact of AFDC on Young Women's Childbearing Decisions." Paper. The Urban Institute, Washington, D.C.

Allen, J.; Philliber, S.; and Hoggson, N. 1990. "School-Based Prevention of teen-Age Pregnancy and School Dropout: Process Evaluation of the National Replication of the Teen Outreach Program." *American Journal of Community Psychology* 18 (4): 505–523.

Anderson, J.E., and Cope, L.G. 1987. "The Impact of Family Planning Program Activity on Fertility." *Family Planning Perspectives* 19:152–157.

Apgar, W.C., and Brown, H.J. 1989. *The State of the Nation's Housing: 1988.* Cambridge, Mass.: The Joint Center for Housing Studies, Harvard University.

Bahr, S.J. 1979. "The Effects of Welfare on Marital Stability and Remarriage." *Journal of Marriage and the Family* 41 (August): 533–560.

Bane, M.J. 1976. *Here to Stay: American Families in the Twentieth Century.* New York: Basic Books.

Bane, M.J., and Ellwood, D.T. 1983. "The Dynamics of Dependency: The Routes to Self-Sufficiency." Cambridge, Mass.: Urban Systems Research and Engineering.

———. 1986. "Slipping Into and Out of Poverty: The Dynamics of Spells." *Journal of Resources* 21 (1): 1–23.

———. 1994. *Welfare Realities: From Rhetoric to Reform.* Cambridge, Mass.: Harvard University Press.

Barnett, W.S. 1992. "Benefits of Compensatory Preschool Education." *Journal of Human Resources* 27 (2): 279–312.

Barnow, B.S. 1987. "The Impact of CETA Programs on Earnings: A Review of the Literature." *Journal of Human Resources* 22 (2): 157–193.

Bassi, L. 1987. "Family Structure and Poverty Among Women and Children:

What Accounts for Change?" Mimeo. Georgetown University, Washington, D.C. June.

Bassi, L.J., and Ashenfelter, O. 1986. "The Effect of Direct Job Creation and Training Programs on Low-Skilled Workers." In *Fighting Poverty: What Works and What Doesn't,* ed. S. Danziger and D.H. Weinberg. Cambridge, Mass.: Harvard University Press.

Beckerman, W. 1979. "The Impact of Income Maintenance Payments on Poverty in Britain, 1975." *Economic Journal* (June): 261–279.

Behn, R.D. 1991. *Leadership Counts: Lessons for Public Managers from Massachusetts Welfare, Training, and Employment Program.* Cambridge, Mass.: Harvard University Press.

Beller, A.H. 1980. "The Effect of Economic Conditions on the Success of Equal Employment Opportunity Laws." *The Review of Economics and Statistics* 62 (August).

———. 1982. "Occupational Segregation by Sex: Determinants and Changes." *Journal of Human Resources* 17 (summer).

Bergman, B. 1974. "Occupational Segregation, Wages and Profits When Employers Discriminate by Race or Sex." *Eastern Economic Journal* 1 (April): 103–110.

———. 1989. "Does the Market for Women's Labor Need Fixing?" *Journal of Economic Perspectives* 3 (winter): 43–60.

Berrueta-Clement, J.R., et al. 1984. *Changed Lives: The Effects of the Perry Preschool Program on Youths Through Age 19.* Ypsilanti, Mich.: High Scope Educational Research Foundation.

Berry, J. 1984. *Feeding Hungry People: Rulemaking in the Food Stamp Program.* New Brunswick, N.J.: Rutgers University Press.

Beyna, L.; Bell, J.; and Trutko, J. 1984. *Six Month Evaluation of the Maryland Day Care Voucher Demonstration.* Arlington, Va.: James Bell and Associates.

Bianchi, S., and Farley, R. 1979. "Racial Differences in Family Living Arrangements and Economic Well-Being: An Analysis of Recent Trends." *Journal of Marriage and the Family* 41 (August): 537–551.

Bishop, J., and Haveman, R. 1979. "Selective Employment Subsidies: Can Okun's Law Be Repealed?" *American Economic Review* (May): 124–130.

Blank, R. 1994. "The Employment Strategy: Public Policies to Increase Work and Earnings." In *Confronting Poverty: Prescriptions for Change,* ed. S. Danziger; G. Sandefur; and D. Weinberg. 168–204. Cambridge, Mass.: Harvard University Press.

Blankenhorn, D. 1994. *Fatherless America: Confronting Our Most Urgent Social Problem.* Dunmore, Pa.: Basic Books.

Blau, D.M., and Robins, P.K. 1988. "Child-Care Costs and Family Labor Supply." *Review of Economics and Statistics* 70 (August): 374–381.

Bloom, H.S.; Orr, L.L.; Cave, G.; Bell, S.; and Doolittle, F. 1993. "The National JTPA Study." Report to the U.S. Department of Labor. Bethesda, Md.: Abt Associates.

Bobo, L., and Smith, R. 1994. "Antipoverty Policy, Affirmative Action, and Racial Attitudes." In *Confronting Poverty: Prescriptions for Change,* ed. S.

Danziger; G. Sandefur; and D. Weinberg. 365–395. Cambridge, Mass.: Harvard University Press.

Bound, J., and Freeman, R. 1992. "What Went Wrong? The Erosion of Relative Earnings and Employment Among Young Black Men in the 1980s." *Quarterly Journal of Economics* 107 (1): 201–232.

Bound, J., and Holzer, H. 1993. "Industrial Structure, Skill Levels, and the Labor Market for White and Black Males." *Review of Economics and Statistics* 75 (3): 387–396.

Bound, J., and Johnson, G. 1992. "Changes in the Structure of Wages: An Evaluation of Alternative Hypotheses." *American Economic Review* 82 (3): 371–392.

Brandon, P. 1995. "Vulnerability to Future Dependence Among Former AFDC Mothers." Discussion paper no. 1055-95. Institute for Research on Poverty, University of Wisconsin, Madison.

Brown, B. 1977. "Long-Term Gains from Early Intervention: An Overview of Current Research." Paper presented at the 1977 annual meeting of the American Association for the Advancement of Science, Denver, Colo.

Bumpass, L. 1984. "Children and Marital Disruption: A Replication and an Update." *Demography* 21 (February): 71–82.

Bumpass, L., and McLanahan, S. 1989. "Unmarried Motherhood: Recent Trends, Composition, and Black-White Differences." *Demography* 26 (May): 279–286.

Bumpass, L., and Raley, R.K. 1993. "Trends in the Duration of Single-Parent Families." National Survey of Families and Households Working Paper no. 58, Center for Demography and Ecology, University of Wisconsin, Madison. May.

Bumpass, L., and Rindfuss, R.R. 1979. "Children and the Experience of Marital Disruption." *American Journal of Sociology* 85 (July): 49–65.

Burlage, D. 1978. "Divorced and Separated Mothers: Combining the Responsibilities of Breadwinning and Child Rearing." Ph.D. diss., Harvard University.

Burstein, P. 1979. "Equal Employment Opportunity Legislation and the Income of Women and Nonwhites." *American Sociological Review* 44 (June): 367–391.

Burt, M. 1986. "Estimates of Public Costs for Teenage Childbearing." Unpublished paper, Center for Population Options, Washington, D.C.

Burtless, G. 1989. "The Effect of Reform on Employment, Earnings and Income." In *Welfare Policy for the 1990s*, ed. P.H. Cottingham and D.T. Ellwood. 103–140. Cambridge, Mass.: Harvard University Press.

———. 1994. "Public Spending on the Poor: Historical Trends and Economic Limits." In *Confronting Poverty: Prescriptions for Change*, ed. S. Danziger; G. Sandefur; and D. Weinberg. 51–84. Cambridge, Mass.: Harvard University Press.

Button, J.W. 1989. *Blacks and Social Change: Impact of the Civil Rights Movement in Southern Communities*. Princeton, N.J.: Princeton University Press.

Cain, G. 1987. "Negative Income Tax Experiments and the Issue of Marital

Stability and Family Composition." In *Lessons from the Income Experiments,* ed. A. Munnell. Boston: Federal Reserve Bank.

Cairncross, F. 1988. "European Countries Vary Widely in Health-Care Delivery Systems." *Financier: The Journal of Private Sector Policy* 12:10–13.

Carlson, E., and Stinson, K. 1982. "Motherhood, Marriage Timing, and Marital Stability: A Research Note." *Social Forces* 61 (September): 258–267.

Carnegie Corporation Report. 1994. New York: Carnegie Corporation.

Casey Foundation. 1995. *Kids Count Data Book.* Baltimore, Md.: Annie E. Casey Foundation.

Chafe, W.H. 1972. *The American Woman: Her Changing Social, Economic and Political Role, 1920–1970.* New York: Oxford University Press.

Chafetz, J.S. 1984. *Sex and Advantage: A Comparative Macro-Structural Theory of Sex Stratification.* Totowa, N.J.: Rowman and Allanheld.

Cherlin, A. 1980. "Postponing Marriage: The Influence of Young Women's Work Expectations." *Journal of Marriage and the Family* 42 (May): 355–365.

———. 1981. *Marriage, Divorce, and Remarriage.* Cambridge, Mass.: Harvard University Press.

Christopher, F.S., and Roosa, M.W. 1990. "An Evaluation of an Adolescent Pregnancy Prevention Program: Is 'Just Say No' Enough?" *Family Relations* 39 (January): 68–72.

Cicirelli, V.G., et al. 1977. *The Impact of Head Start: An Evaluation of the Effects of Head Start on Children's Cognitive and Affective Development.* Columbus: Westinghouse Learning Corporation, Ohio University.

Citizens' Board of Inquiry into Hunger and Malnutrition in the United States. 1968. *Hunger, USA.* Boston: Beacon.

Clayton, R.R., and Voss, H.L. 1977. "Shacking Up: Cohabitation in the 1970s." *Journal of Marriage and the Family* 39 (May): 273–283.

Cocoran, M., and Duncan, G. 1979. "Work History, Labor Force Attachment, and Earnings Differences between Races and Sexes." *Journal of Human Resources* 14 (1): 3–20.

Commission of the European Communities. 1981. *Final Report from the Commissioner to the Council on the First Programme of Pilot Scheme and Studies to Combat Poverty.* Brussels.

Committee for Economic Development. 1989. *Children in Need: Investment Strategies for the Educationally Disadvantaged.* Washington, D.C.: CED.

Congressional Quarterly Weekly Report. 1995. "House GOP Welfare Plan Shifts Focus from Work to Teen Mothers." Vol. 53, no. 2:160.

Consortium for Longitudinal Studies. 1978. *Lasting Effects After Preschool.* Final Report of DHEW Grant no. 90C-1311. Washington, D.C.: U.S. Administration for Children, Youth, and Families.

Cook, A.H. 1989. "Public Policies to Help Dual-Earner Families Meet the Demands of the Work World." *Industrial and Labor Relations Review* 48:201–215.

Cooney, R.S. 1979. "Demographic Components of Growth in White, Black and Puerto Rican Female-Headed Families: Comparison of the Cutright and Ross Sawhill Methodologies." *Social Research* 8 (June): 144–158.

Cottingham, C., ed. 1982. *Race, Poverty, and the Urban Underclass.* Lexington, Mass.: Lexington Books.

Cottingham, P.H., and Ellwood, D.T., eds. 1989. *Welfare Policy for the 1990s.* Cambridge, Mass.: Harvard University Press.

Cramer, J.C. 1980. "Fertility and Female Employment." *American Sociological Review* 47 (August): 556–567.

Cutler, D., and Katz, L. 1992. "Rising Inequality? Changes in the Distribution of Income and Consumption in the 1980s." *American Economic Review* 82:546–551.

Cutright, P. 1974. "Components of Change in the Number of Female Family Heads Aged 15–44: U.S., 1940–70." *Journal of Marriage and the Family* 36 (November): 714–721.

Danziger, S. 1982. "Children in Poverty: The Truly Needy Who Fall Through the Safety Net." *Children and Youth Service* 10 (2): 35–51.

———. 1989. "Fighting Poverty and Reducing Welfare Dependency." In *Welfare Policies for the 1990s,* ed. P.H. Cottingham and D.T. Ellwood. 41–69. Cambridge, Mass.: Harvard University Press.

Danziger, S., and Gottschalk, P. 1985. "The Poverty of Losing Ground." *Challenge* 28 (May–June): 32–38.

———. 1988–1989. "Increasing Inequality in the United States: What We Know and What We Don't." *Journal of Post Keynesian Economics* 11 (2): 174–195.

Danziger, S.; Gottschalk, P.; and Smolensky, E. 1989. "How the Rich Have Fared, 1973–1987." *The American Economic Review* 79 (May): 310–314.

Danziger, S., and Haveman, R. 1981. "The Reagan Administration's Budget Cuts: Their Impact on the Poor." *Challenge* 24 (May–June): 5–13.

Danziger, S.; Jakubson, G.; Schwartz, S.; and Smolensky, E. 1982. "Work and Welfare as Determinants of Female Poverty and Household Headship." *Quarterly Journal of Economics* 98:519–534.

Danziger, S.; Sandefur, G.; and Weinberg, D., eds. 1994. *Confronting Poverty: Prescriptions for Change.* Cambridge, Mass.: Harvard University Press.

Danziger, S., and Weinberg, D. 1994. "The Historical Record: Trends in Family Income, Inequality and Poverty." In *Confronting Poverty: Prescriptions for Change,* ed. S. Danziger; G. Sandefur; and D. Weinberg. 18–50. Cambridge, Mass.: Harvard University Press.

Dechter, A., and Smock, P. 1994. "The Fading Breadwinner Role and the Implications for Young Couples." Discussion paper no. 1051-94. Institute for Research on Poverty, University of Wisconsin, Madison.

DeSario, J.P., ed. 1989. *International Public Policy Sourcebook.* Westport, Conn.: Greenwood Press.

Downes, B.T. 1968. "Social and Political Characteristics of Riot Cities: A Comparative Study." *Social Science Quarterly* 49 (December): 509–520.

Dubnoff, S. 1986. "Work Related Day Care: A Survey of Parents." *FY '86 Day Care Report.* Boston: Massachusetts Department of Social Services.

Duncan, G.J., and Hoffman, S.D. 1988. "Welfare Dependence Within and Across Generations." *Science* 239:467–471.

Duncan, G.J., and Ponza, M. 1987. "Public Attitudes Toward the Structure of Income Maintenance Programs." Working paper, Survey Research Center, University of Michigan, Ann Arbor.

Duncan, G.J., and Rodgers, W.L. 1991. "Has Children's Poverty Become More Persistent?" *American Sociological Review* 56:538–550.

Duvall, L.J.; Gondreau, D.W.; and Marsh, R.E. 1982. "Aid to Families with Dependent Children: Characteristics of Recipients in 1979." *Social Security Bulletin* 45 (April): 1, 6.

Easterlin, R. 1980. *Birth and Fortune: The Impact of Numbers on Personal Wealth.* New York: Basic Books.

Ellwood, D.T. 1986. "Targeting Would-Be Long-Term Recipients of AFDC." Princeton, N.J.: Mathematica Policy Research Inc.

———. 1988. *Poor Support: Poverty in the American Family.* New York: Basic Books.

———. 1989. "Conclusions." In *Welfare Policy for the 1990s,* ed. P.H. Cottingham and D.T. Ellwood. 269–290. Cambridge, Mass.: Harvard University Press.

Ellwood, D.T., and Bane, M.J. 1985. "The Impact of AFDC on Family Structure and Living Arrangements." *Research in Labor Economics* 7:137–149.

Ellwood, D.T., and Crane, J. 1990. "Family Change Among Black Americans." *Journal of Economic Perspectives* 4 (fall): 65–84.

Ellwood, D.T., and Rodda, D.T. 1991. "The Hazards of Work and Marriage: The Influence of Male Employment on Marriage Rates." Working paper, John F. Kennedy School of Government, Harvard University.

Espenshade, T.J. 1979. "The Economic Consequences of Divorce." *Journal of Marriage and Family* 41 (August): 615–625.

Evanson, E. 1984. "Employment Programs for the Poor: Government in the Labor Market." *Focus* 7 (fall): 1–7.

Feagin, J.R. 1975. *Subordinating the Poor: Welfare and American Beliefs.* Englewood Cliffs, N.J.: Prentice-Hall.

Fester, D.; Gottschalk, P.; and Jakubson, G. 1984. "Impact of OBRA on AFDC Recipients in Wisconsin." Discussion paper no. 763-84 (November). Madison, Wisc.: Institute for Research on Poverty.

Finer, M., et al. 1974. *Report on the Committee on One-Parent Families.* London: Her Majesty's Stationery Office.

Flora, P., and Heidenheimer, A.J., eds. 1981. *The Development of Welfare States in Europe and America.* New Brunswick, N.J.: Transaction.

Ford Foundation. 1989. *The Common Good: Social Welfare and the American Future.* New York: Ford Foundation.

Forest, J.D.; Hermalin, A.I.; and Henshaw, S.K. 1981. "The Impact of Family Planning Clinic Programs on Adolescent Pregnancy." *Family Planning Perspectives* 13:3–12.

Fosburg, S., and Hawkins, P. 1981. *Final Report of the National Day Care Home Study.* Vol. 1. Cambridge, Mass.: Abt Books.

Freeman, J. 1975. *The Politics of Women's Liberation.* New York: Longman.

Friedlander, D.; Erickson, M.; Hamilton, G.; and Knox, V. 1986. *West Vir-*

ginia: Final Report on the Community Work Experience Demonstration. New York: Manpower Demonstration Research Corporation.

Friedlander, D.; Freedman, S.; Hamilton, G.; and Quint, J. 1987. *Final Report on the Illinois WIN Demonstration Program in Cook County.* New York: Manpower Demonstration Research Corporation.

Friedlander, D.; Hoerz, G.; Long, D.; and Quint, J. 1985. *Maryland: Final Report on the Employment Initiatives Evaluation.* New York: Manpower Demonstration Research Corporation.

Friedlander, D., and Long, D. 1987. *A Study of Performance Measures and Subgroup Impacts in Three Welfare Employment Programs.* New York: Manpower Demonstration Research Corporation.

Friedman, D.E. 1986. "Child Care For Employees' Kids." *Harvard Business Review* (March–April): 28–34.

Fuchs, V. 1981. *How We Live.* Cambridge, Mass: Harvard University Press.

———. 1989. "Women's Quest for Economic Equality." *Journal of Economic Perspectives* 3 (winter): 25–41.

Furniss, N., and Mitchell, N. 1984. "Social Welfare Provisions in Western Europe: Current Status and Future Possibilities." In *Public Policy and Social Institutions,* ed. H. Rodgers. Greenwich, Conn.: JAI Press.

Furniss, N., and Tilton, T. 1979. *The Case for the Welfare State: From Social Security to Social Equality.* Bloomington: Indiana University Press.

Furstenberg, F.F., Jr. 1976. *Unplanned Parenthood: The Social Consequences of Teenage Childbearing.* New York: Free Press.

Furstenberg, F.F., Jr.; Lincoln, R.; and Menken, J. 1981. *Teenage Sexuality, Pregnancy, and Childbearing.* Philadelphia: University of Pennsylvania Press.

Gamble, T., and Zigler, E. 1985. "Effects of Infant Day Care: Another Look at the Evidence." *American Journal of Orthopsychiatry* 56:26–42.

Garfinkel, I. 1992. *Assuring Child Support: An Extension of Social Security.* New York: Russell Sage Foundation.

Garfinkel I., and McLanahan, S. 1986. *Single Mothers and Their Children: A New American Dilemma.* Washington, D.C.: Urban Institute.

———. 1994. "Single-Mother Families, Economic Security, and Government Policy." In *Confronting Poverty: Prescriptions for Change,* ed. S. Danziger; G. Sandefur; and D. Weinberg. 205–225. Cambridge, Mass.: Harvard University Press.

Garfinkel, I.; McLanahan, S.; and Wong, P. 1988. "Child Support and Dependency." In *Beyond Welfare: New Approaches to the Problem of Poverty in America,* ed. H.R. Rodgers Jr. Armonk, N.Y.: M.E. Sharpe.

Garfinkel, I., and Melli, M. 1982. "Child Support: Weakness of the Old and Features of a Proposed New System." Special report nos. 32A, 32B, 32C, Institute for Research on Poverty, University of Wisconsin, Madison.

Garfinkel, I.; Melli, M.; and Robertson, J. 1994. *The Future of Children.* Vol. 4, no. 1:84–100. Madison, Wisc.: Center for the Future of Children, David and Lucile Packard Foundation.

Garfinkel, I., and Uhr, E. 1984. "A New Approach to Child Support." *Public Interest* 75 (spring): 111–122.

Gilder, G. 1981. *Wealth and Poverty*. New York: Bantam.

Ginsburg, H. 1983. *Full Employment and Public Policy: The United States and Sweden*. Lexington, Mass.: Lexington Books.

Glick, P.C., and Spanier, G.B. 1980. "Married and Unmarried Cohabitation in the United States." *Journal of Marriage and the Family* 42 (February): 19–30.

Gold, M.E. 1983. *A Dialogue on Comparable Worth*. New York: ILR Press, New York State School of Industrial and Labor Relations, Cornell University.

Goldman, B.; Friedlander, D.; and Long, D. 1986. *Final Report on the San Diego Job Search and Work Experience Demonstration*. New York: Manpower Demonstration Research Corporation.

Gottschalk, P. 1981. "Transfer Scenarios and Projections of Poverty into the 1980s." *Journal of Human Resources* 16:41–60.

Gottschalk, P.; McLanahan, S.; and Sandefur, G. 1994. "The Dynamics and Intergenerational Transmission of Poverty and Welfare Participation." In *Confronting Poverty: Prescriptions for Change*, ed. S. Danziger; G. Sandefur; and D. Weinberg. 85–108. Cambridge, Mass.: Harvard University Press.

Gottschalk, P., and Moffitt, R. 1994. "The Growth of Earnings Instability in the U.S. Labor Market." *Brookings Papers on Economic Activity*, no. 2:217–272.

Gramlich, E. 1986. "Evaluation of Educational Projects: The Case of the Perry Pre-School Program." *Economics of Education Review* 5:17–24.

Grant Foundation. 1988a. *The Forgotten Half: Non-College Youth in America*. Washington, D.C.: W.T. Grant Foundation.

———. 1988b. *The Forgotten Half: Pathways to Success for America's Youth and Young Families*. Washington, D.C.: W.T. Grant Foundation.

Greenberg, D.; Meyer, R.; and Wiseman, M. 1994. "Multisite Employment and Training Program Evaluations: A Tale of Three Studies." *Industrial and Labor Relations Review* 47 (4): 679–691.

Groeneveld, L.; Hannan, T.; and Tuma, N. 1983. "Marital Stability." *Final Report of the Seattle/Denver Income Maintenance Experiment*. Vol. 1: *Design and Results*. Washington, D.C.: GPO.

Gueron, J.M. 1986. *Work Initiatives for Welfare Recipients: Lessons from a Multi-State Experience*. New York: Manpower Demonstration Research Corporation.

———. 1987. *Reforming Welfare with Work*. New York: Russell Sage Foundation.

Gueron, J.M., and Pauly, E. 1991. *From Welfare to Work*. New York: Russell Sage Foundation.

Gutmann, A., ed. 1988. *Democracy and the Welfare State*. Princeton, N.J.: Princeton University Press.

Guttentag, M., and Secord, P. 1983. *Too Many Women: The Sex Ratio Question*. Beverly Hills, Calif.: Sage.

Haanes-Olsen, L. 1989. "Worldwide Trends and Developments in Social Security, 1985–87." *Social Security Bulletin* 52, no. 2. Washington, D.C.: Department of Health and Human Services.

Hahn, L.H., and Feagin, J.R. 1970. "Rank-and-File Versus Congressional Perceptions of Ghetto Riots." *Social Science Quarterly* 51 (September): 361–373.

Hallett, G., ed. 1988. *Land and Housing Policies in Europe and the USA: A Comparative Analysis.* New York: Routledge.

Hannan, M.T.; Tuma, N.B.; and Groeneveld, P. 1977. "Income and Marital Events: Evidence from the Income Maintenance Experiment." *American Journal of Sociology* 82 (May): 1186–1211.

Hanson, R.L. 1983. "The 'Content' of Welfare Policy: The States and Aid to Families with Dependent Children." *Journal of Politics* 45:771–785.

———. 1984. "Medicaid and the Politics of Redistribution." *American Journal of Political Science* 28:313–339.

Harvey, P. 1989. *Securing the Right to Employment: Social Welfare Policy and the Unemployed in the United States.* Princeton, N.J.: Princeton University Press.

Haveman, R., and Scholz, J. 1994. "The Clinton Welfare Reform Plan: Will It End Poverty As We Know It?" Discussion paper no. 1037-94. Institute for Research on Poverty, University of Wisconsin, Madison.

Hayes, C., ed. 1987. *Risking the Future: Adolescent Sexuality, Pregnancy, and Childbearing.* Washington, D.C.: National Academy Press.

Headey, B. 1978. *Housing Policy in the Developed Economy: The United Kingdom, Sweden, and the United States.* London: Croom Helm.

Heclo, H. 1994. "Poverty Politics." In *Confronting Poverty: Prescriptions for Change,* ed. S. Danziger; G. Sandefur; and D. Weinberg. 396–437. Cambridge, Mass.: Harvard University Press.

Helburn, S., et al. 1995. "Cost, Quality and Child Care Outcomes in Child Care Centers." Paper. University of Colorado, Boulder.

Hertzke, A.D., and Scribner, M.K. 1989. "The Politics of Federal Day Care: The Nexus of Family, Church, and the Positive State." Prepared for delivery at the annual meeting of the American Political Science Association, Atlanta, August 31, 1989.

Hofferth, S., and Moore, K. 1979. "Early Childbearing and Later Economic Well-Being." *American Sociological Review* 44 (October): 784–815.

Hofferth, S., and Phillips, D.A. 1987. "Child Care in the United States: 1970 to 1985." *Journal of Marriage and Family* 49: 559–571.

Holden, K.C., and Smock, P.J. 1991. "The Economic Costs of Marital Dissolution: Why Do Women Bear a Disproportionate Cost?" *Annual Review of Sociology* 17:51–78.

Hollister, R.G.; Kemper, P.; and Maynard, R.A., eds. 1984. *The National Supported Work Demonstration.* Madison: University of Wisconsin Press.

Hoynes, H., and MaCurdy, T. 1994. "Has the Decline in Benefits Shortened Welfare Spells?" *American Economic Review* 84:43–48.

Jackson, J.J. 1973. "Black Women in a Racist Society." In *Racism and Mental Health,* ed. C.V. Willie; B.M. Kramer; and B.S. Brown. Pittsburgh: University of Pittsburgh Press.

Jencks, C. 1992. *Rethinking Social Policy: Race, Poverty and the Underclass.* New York: Harper-Perennial.

Jones, E.F., et al. 1985. "Teenage Pregnancy in Developed Countries: Determinants and Policy Implications." *Family Planning Perspectives* 17 (March–April): 53–63.

Juhn, C. 1992. "The Decline of Male Labor Force Participation: The Role of Declining Market Opportunities." Paper. Department of Economics, University of Chicago.

Kahn, A.J. 1983. *Income Transfers for Families with Children: An Eight-County Study.* Philadelphia: Temple University Press.

———. 1987. *Child Care: Facing the Hard Choices.* Dover, Mass.: Auburn House.

———. 1988. *Child Support: From Debt Collection to Social Policy.* Beverly Hills, Calif.: Sage.

Kakwani, N., and Subbarao, K. 1994. "Global Development: Is the Gap Widening or Closing?" In *Poverty Policy in Developing Nations,* ed. T. DeGregori and H. Rodgers. 65–118. Greenwich, Conn.: JAI Press.

Kamerman, S.B. 1980. *Maternity and Parental Benefits and Leaves: An International Review.* New York: Columbia University Press.

———. 1984. "Women, Children and Poverty: Public Policies and Female-Headed Families in Industrialized Countries." *Signs: Journal of Women in Culture and Society* 10 (21): 249–271.

———. 1988. *Mothers Alone: Strategies for a Time of Change.* Dover, Mass.: Auburn House.

———. 1989. *Privatization and the Welfare State.* Princeton, N.J.: Princeton University Press.

———. 1991. "Child Care Policies and Programs: An International Overview." *Journal of Social Issues* 47 (2): 179–196.

Kamerman, S.B., and Kahn, A.J. 1981. *Child Care, Family Benefits, and Working Parents.* New York: Columbia University Press.

———. 1983. "Child Support: Some International Developments." In *Parental Support Obligations,* ed. J. Cassetty. Lexington, Mass.: Lexington Books.

———. 1987. Quoted in *Ms.,* March, 44.

———. 1988. "What Europe Does for Single-Parent Families." *Public Interest* (fall): 70–86.

Katz, M.B. 1986. *In the Shadow of the Poorhouse: A Social History of Welfare in America.* New York: Basic Books.

Kessler-Harris, A. 1982. *Out to Work—A History of Wage-Earning Women in the United States.* New York: Oxford University Press.

Ketron, Inc. 1980. *The Long-Term Impact of WIN II: A Longitudinal Evaluation of the Employment Experiences of Participants in the Work Incentive Program.* Report. Wayne, Pa.: Ketron, Inc.

Keyserling, M. 1972. *Windows on Day Care.* New York: National Council of Jewish Women.

Kim, R.; Garfinkel, I.; and Meyer, D. 1994. "Interaction Effects of a Child Tax Credit, National Health Insurance, and Assured Child Support." Discussion paper no. 1047-94. Institute for Research on Poverty, University of Wisconsin, Madison.

Kimmich, M. 1984. *Children's Services in the Reagan Era.* Washington, D.C.: Urban Institute.

King, A.G. 1978. "Labor Market Racial Discrimination Against Black Women." *The Review of Black Political Economy* 8 (summer): 116–131.

Korbin, K.E. 1973. "Household Headship and Its Changes in the United States, 1940–1960, 1970." *Journal of the American Statistical Association* 68 (December): 793–800.

Korenman, S.; Miller, J.E.; and Sjaastad, J.E. 1994. *Long-term Poverty and Child Development in the United States: Results from the NLSY Child Youth Services Review.* Special issue on Child Poverty and Social Policies.

Kotz, N. 1971. *Let Them Eat Promises: The Politics of Hunger in America.* New York: Doubleday.

———. 1979. *Hunger in America: The Federal Response.* New York: Field Foundation.

Kristof, N. 1995. "Japanese Investment: Good Day Care." *New York Times,* 1 February: A4.

Lantz, H.; Martin, S.; and O'Hara, M. 1977. "The Changing American Family from the Preindustrial to the Industrial Period: A Final Report." *American Sociological Review* 42 (June): 406–421.

LeCompte, M.D., and Dworkin, A.G. 1988. "Educational Programs: Indirect Linkages and Unfulfilled Expectations." In *Beyond Welfare: New Approaches to the Problem of Poverty in America,* ed. H.R. Rodgers Jr. 135–167. Armonk, N.Y.: M.E. Sharpe.

Leichter, H.M. 1979. *A Comparative Approach to Policy Analysis: Health Care Policy in Four Nations.* New York: Cambridge University Press.

Leichter, H.M., and Rodgers, H.R., Jr. 1984. *American Public Policy in a Comparative Context.* New York: McGraw-Hill.

Leman, C. 1977. "Patterns of Policy Development: Social Security in the United States and Canada." *Public Policy* 25 (spring): 261–291.

Leonard, P.A.; Dolbeare, C.N.; and Lazere, E.B. 1989. *A Place to Call Home: The Crisis in Housing for the Poor.* Washington, D.C.: Center on Budget and Policy Priorities and Low Income Housing Information Service.

Leonard, P., and Greenstein, R. 1993. *The New Budget Reconciliation Law: Progressive Deficit Retention and Critical Social Investments.* Washington, D.C.: Center on Budget and Policy Priorities.

Lerman, R.I. 1989. "Child-Support Policies." In *Welfare Policy for the 1990s,* ed. P.H. Cottingham and D.T. Ellwood. 219–247. Cambridge, Mass.: Harvard University Press.

Levitan, S.; Rein, M.; and Marwick, D. 1972. *Work and Welfare Go Together.* Baltimore: Johns Hopkins Press.

Levy, F. 1980. "Labor Force Dynamics and the Distribution of Employability." Washington, D.C.: Urban Institute.

Lichter, D.; McLaughlin, D.; Kephart, G.; and Landry, D. 1992. "Race and the Retreat from Marriage: A Shortage of Marriageable Men?" *American Sociological Review* 56:15–32.

Lindbeck, A. 1988. "Consequences of the Advanced Welfare State." *World Economy* 11:19–37.

Lloyd, C.B., and Niemi, B.T. 1979. *The Economics of Sex Differentials.* New York: Columbia University Press.

Long, D.; Wood, R.; and Koop, H. 1994. *LEAP: The Educational Effects of LEAP and Enhanced Services in Cleveland.* New York: Manpower Demonstration Research Corporation.

McGuire, C.C. 1981. *International Housing Policies: A Comparative Analysis.* Lexington, Mass.: Lexington Books.

McLanahan, S. 1985. "Family Structure and the Reproduction of Poverty." *American Journal of Sociology* 90 (4): 873–901.

———. 1988. "Intergenerational Consequences of Family Disruptions." *American Journal of Sociology* 94 (July): 130–152.

Magid, R.Y. 1983. *Child Care Initiatives for Working Parents: Why Employers Get Involved.* New York: American Management Association.

Magnet, M. 1993. *The Dream and the Nightmare: The Sixties' Legacy to the Underclass.* New York: William Morrow.

Mahler, V.A., and Claudio, J.K. 1988. "Social Benefits in Advanced Capitalist Countries: A Cross-National Comparison." *Comparative Politics* 21:37–51.

Mahler, V.A., and Katz, C.J. 1988. "Social Benefits in Advanced Capitalist Countries." *Comparative Politics* 43:37–51.

Mallar, C., et al. 1984. *The Lasting Impact of Job Corps Participation.* Princeton, N.J.: Mathematica.

Mann, A.J. 1977. "A Review of Head Start Research Since 1969." Paper presented at the 1977 annual meeting of the American Association for the Advancement of Science, Denver.

Manpower Demonstration Research Corporation. 1980. *Summary and Findings of the National Supported Work Demonstration.* New York: Ballinger.

———. 1985. "Job Start: Report One." New York: Manpower Demonstration Research Corporation.

Mare, R., and Winship, C. 1991. "Socioeconomic Change and the Decline of Marriage for Blacks and Whites." In *The Urban Underclass,* ed. C. Jenks and P. Peterson. Washington, D.C.: Brookings Institute.

Martinson, K., and Friedlander, D. 1994. *GAIN: Basic Education in a Welfare-to-Work Program.* New York: Manpower Demonstration Research Corporation.

Mead, L.M. 1986. *Beyond Entitlement: The Social Obligations of Citizenship.* New York: Free Press.

Miller, A.C. 1975. "Health Care of Children and Youth in America." *American Journal of Public Health* 65 (April): 353–358.

Miller, T.I. 1984. "The Effects of Employer Sponsored Child Care on Employee Absenteeism, Turnover, Productivity, Recruitment or Job Satisfaction: What Is Claimed and What Is Known." *Personnel Psychology* 37:277–289.

Moffitt, R. 1992. "Incentive Effects of the U.S. Welfare System: A Review." *Journal of Economic Literature* 30 (March): 1–61.

Moffitt, R., and Wolf, D.A. 1987. "The Effect of the 1981 Omnibus Budget Reconciliation Act on Welfare Recipients and Work Incentives." *Social Service Review* 61:247–260.

Moles, O.C. 1979. "Public Welfare Payments and Marital Dissolution: A Review of Recent Studies." In *Divorce and Separation: Context, Causes, and Consequences,* ed. G. Levinger and O.C. Moles. New York: Basic Books.

Moore, K., and Burt, M. 1981. *Teenage Childbearing and Welfare: Policy Perspectives on Sexual Activity, Pregnancy, and Public Dependency.* Washington, D.C.: Urban Institute.

Moore, K., and Caldwell, S. 1976. *Out-of-Wedlock Pregnancy and Childbearing.* Washington, D.C.: Urban Institute.

———. 1977. "The Effect of Government Policies on Out-of-Wedlock Sex and Pregnancy." *Family Planning Perspective* 9 (July–August): 71–93.

Moore, K., and Waite, L. 1981. "Marital Dissolution, Early Motherhood and Early Marriage." *Social Forces* 60 (September): 20–40.

Moscovice, I., and Craig, W. 1983. "The Impact of Federal Cutbacks on Working AFDC Recipients in Minnesota." Discussion paper. University of Minnesota, Minneapolis. December.

Mulroy, E.A., ed. 1988. *Women as Single Parents: Confronting Institutional Barriers in the Courts, the Workplace, and the Housing Market.* Dover, Mass.: Auburn House.

Murnane, R. 1994. "Education and the Well-Being of the Next Generation." In *Confronting Poverty: Prescriptions for Change,* ed. S. Danziger; G. Sandefur; and D. Weinberg. 289–307. Cambridge, Mass.: Harvard University Press.

Murphy, I.L. 1973. *Public Policy on the Status of Women.* Lexington, Mass.: Heath.

Murray, C. 1984. *Losing Ground: American Social Policy.* New York: Basic Books.

National Center for Health Statistics. 1993. "Advance Report of Final Natality Statistics, 1991." *U.S. Monthly Vital Statistics Report* 41, no. 9.

National Committee on Pay Equity. 1984. *Who's Working for Working Women.* Washington, D.C.: GPO.

National Forum Foundation. 1985. *Child Support Enforcement: Unequal Protection Under the Law.* Washington, D.C.

Navarro, V. 1989. "Why Some Countries Have National Health Insurance, Others Have National Health Services, and the U.S. Has Neither." *Social Science and Medicine* 28:887–898.

Nichols-Casebolt, A., and Garfinkel, I. 1991. "Trends in Paternity Adjudications and Child Support Awards." *Social Science Quarterly* 72:83–97.

Oaxaca, R. 1973. "Male-Female Wage Differentials in Urban Labor Markets." *International Economic Review* 14:693–709.

OECD. 1976. *Public Expenditures on Income Maintenance Programmes.* Paris: OECD.

———. 1988. *Aging Populations—The Social Policy Implications.* Paris: OECD.

Oellerich, D., and Garfinkel I. 1983. "Distributional Impacts of Existing and

Alternative Child Support Systems." *Policy Studies Journal* 12 (September): 119–129.

Office of Economic Research. 1981. *U.S. Economic Performance in a Global Perspective*. New York: New York Stock Exchange.

Office of Technology Assessment. 1992. *Technologies and the American Economic Transition: Choices for the Future*. OTA-TET–238. Washington, D.C.: GPO.

Oxley, H., and Martin, J. 1991. "Controlling Government Spending and Deficits: Trends in the 1980s and Prospects for the 1990s." *OECD Economic Studies* 17 (autumn): 145–189.

Pavetti, L. 1993. "The Dynamics of Welfare and Work: Exploring the Process by Which Women Work Their Way Off Welfare." Ph.D. diss., Harvard University.

Pearce, D. 1978. "The Feminization of Poverty: Women, Work and Welfare." *Urban and Social Change Review* 3:1–4.

Perlman, S. 1984. *Nobody's Baby: The Politics of Adolescent Pregnancy*. Doctoral diss., Florence Heller School for Advanced Studies in Social Welfare, Brandeis University.

Perloff, J.M., and Wachter, M.L. 1979. "The New Jobs Tax Credit: An Evaluation of the 1977–1978 Wage Subsidy Program." *American Economic Review* 69 (2): 173–179.

Perry, K.S. 1982. *Employers and Child Care: Establishing Services Through the Workplace*. Washington, D.C.: Women's Bureau, U.S. Department of Labor.

Piven, F.F., and Cloward, R.A. 1971. *Regulating the Poor: The Functions of Public Welfare*. New York: Vintage Books.

———. 1979. *Poor People's Movements: Why They Succeed, How They Fail*. New York: Random House.

Plotnick, R.D. 1989. "Welfare and Out-of-Wedlock Childbearing: Evidence from the 1980s." Discussion paper no. 876-89. Madison, Wisc.: Institute for Research on Poverty.

———. 1992. "The Effects of Attitudes on Teenage Premarital Pregnancy and Its Resolution." *American Sociological Review* 57 (December): 800–811.

Polachek, S.W. 1979. "Occupational Segregation Among Women: Theory, Evidence, and a Prognosis." In *Women in the Labor Market*, ed. C.B. Lloyd. New York: Columbia University Press.

Polit, D.F., and O'Hara, J. 1989. "Support Services." In *Welfare Policies for the 1990s*, ed. P.H. Cottingham and D.T. Ellwood. 165–198. Cambridge, Mass.: Harvard University Press.

Postrado, L., and Nicholson, H. 1992. "Effectiveness in Delaying the Initiation of Sexual Intercourse of Girls Aged 12–14." *Youth and Society* 23 (3): 356–379.

Rank, M.R. 1989. "Fertility Among Women on Welfare: Incidence and Determinants." *American Sociological Review* (April): 296–304.

Reischauer, R.D. 1989. "The Welfare Reform Legislation: Directions for the Future." In *Welfare Policies for the 1990s*, ed. P.H. Cottingham and D.T. Ellwood. Cambridge, Mass.: Harvard University Press.

Remick, H., ed. 1981. *Comparable Worth and Wage Discrimination.* Philadelphia: Temple University Press.

Rivlin, A.M. 1984. "Helping the Poor." In *Economic Choices: 1984,* ed. A.M. Rivlin. Washington, D.C.: Brookings Institution.

Robins, P. 1986. "Child Support, Welfare Dependency, and Poverty." *American Economic Review* (September): 768–788.

———. 1988. "Federal Support for Child Care: Current Policies and a Proposed New System." *Challenge* 11 (2): 1–9.

Rodgers, H.R., Jr. 1978. "Hiding versus Ending Poverty." *Politics and Society* 8:253–266.

———. 1979. *Poverty amid Plenty: A Political and Economic Analysis.* Reading, Mass.: Addison-Wesley.

———. 1982. *The Cost of Human Neglect: America's Welfare Failure.* Armonk, N.Y.: M.E. Sharpe.

———. 1985. "Youth and Poverty: An Empirical Test of the Impact of Family Demographics and Race." *Youth and Society* 16 (4): 421–437.

———. 1987a. "Black Americans and the Feminization of Poverty: The Intervening Effects of Unemployment." *Journal of Black Studies* 17 (4): 402–417.

———. 1987b. "The Feminization of Poverty: Some Preliminary Empirical Explorations." *Western Sociological Review* 15 (1): 1–32.

Roemer, M. 1977. *Comparative National Policies on Health Care.* New York: Marcel Dekker.

Roosa, M.W., and Christopher, F.S. 1990. "Evaluation of an Abstinance-Only Adolescent Pregnancy Prevention Program: A Replication." *Family Relations* 39 (October): 363–367.

Rosengren, B. 1973. *Pre-School in Sweden.* Stockholm: Swedish Institute.

Ross, H.L., and Sawhill, I. 1975. *Time of Transition: The Growth of Families Headed by Women.* Washington, D.C.: Urban Institute.

Ruggles, P. 1990. *Drawing the Line: Alternative Poverty Measures and Their Implications for Public Policy.* Washington, D.C.: Urban Institute.

Rytina, N.F. 1982. "Tenure as a Factor in the Male-Female Earnings Gap." *Monthly Labor Review* (April): 32–34.

Sampson, R.J. 1987. "Urban Black Violence: The Effects of Male Joblessness and Family Disruption." *American Journal of Sociology* 93 (September): 348–382.

Sawhill, I. 1988. "Poverty in the U.S.: Why Is It So Persistent?" *Journal of Economic Literature* 26 (September): 1073–1119.

Scales, P. 1983. "Adolescent Sexuality and Education: Principles, Approaches, and Resources." In *Adolescent Sexuality in a Changing American Society,* ed. C.S. Chihman. 207–229. New York: John Wiley & Sons.

Scharf, K.R. 1979. "Teenage Pregnancy: Why the Epidemic?" *Working Papers for a New Society* 6 (March–April): 1–22.

Scholz, J. 1994. "The Earned Income Tax Credit: Participation, Compliance, and Anti-poverty Effectiveness." *National Tax Journal* 47 (1): 59–81.

Schorr, L. 1988. *Within Our Reach: Breaking the Cycle of Disadvantage.* New York: Anchor Press/Doubleday.

Schweinhart, L.J., and Weikart, D.P. 1980. *Effects of Early Childhood Intervention on Teenage Youth: The Perry Preschool Project, 1962–1980.* Monographs of the High/Scope Educational Research Foundation, no. 7.

Scoll, B., and Engstrom, R. 1985. "Final Report of the Hennepin County Grant Purchase of Child Day Care Through a Voucher System." Minneapolis: Hennepin County Community Services Department.

Seltzer, J. 1994. "Consequences of Marital Dissolution for Children." *Annual Review of Sociology* 20:235–266.

Sexton, P. 1977. *Women and Work.* Washington, D.C.: Department of Labor, Employment and Training Administration, Research and Development Corporation.

Shapiro, R.Y.; Patterson, K.D.; Russell, J.; and Young, J.T. 1987. "The Polls: Public Assistance." *Public Opinion Quarterly* 51 (spring): 120–130.

Shram, S.F., and Turbot, J.P. 1983. "Civil Disorder and the Welfare Explosion." *American Sociological Review* 76 (November): 426–442.

Simanis, J.G., and Coleman, J.R. 1980. "Health Care Expenditures in Nine Industrial Countries." *Social Security Bulletin* 43 (January): 3–8.

Smeeding, T. 1992. "Why the U.S. Antipoverty System Doesn't Work Very Well." *Challenge* 35 (January–February): 30–35.

Smeeding, T., and Rainwater, L. 1991. "Cross-National Trends in Income Poverty and Dependency: The Evidence for Young Adults in the Eighties." Paper presented at the Joint Center for Political and Economic Studies, Washington, D.C., September 20–21.

Smith, J.P., and Ward, M. 1989. "Women in the Labor Market and in the Family." *Journal of Economic Perspectives* 3 (winter): 9–23.

Smith, R.E., ed. 1979. *The Subtle Revolution: Women at Work.* Washington, D.C.: Urban Institute.

Smith-Loving, L., and Tickamyer, A. 1978. "Nonrecursive Models of Labor Force Participation, Fertility Behavior, and Sex Role Attitudes." *American Sociological Review* 43 (August): 541–556.

———. 1982. "Models of Fertility and Women's Work." (Comment on Cramer 1980.) *American Sociological Review* 47 (August): 561–566.

Smolensky, E. 1985. "Is a Golden Age in Poverty Policy Right Around the Corner?" *Focus* 8 (spring): 9–11.

Snow, C.; Barnes, W.; Chandler, J.; Hemphill, L.; and Goodman, I. 1991. *Unfulfilled Expectations: Home and School Influences on Literacy.* Cambridge, Mass.: Harvard University Press.

Social Security Administration. 1982. *1979 Recipient Characteristics Study, Part 2: Financial Circumstances of AFDC Families.* Washington, D.C.: GPO.

———. 1983. "Monthly Benefit Statistics." No. 11. Washington, D.C.: GPO.

———. 1985. *Social Security Bulletin* 48 (July). Washington, D.C.: GPO.

———. 1988a. *Social Security Bulletin, Annual Statistical Supplement.* Washington, D.C.: GPO.

———. 1988b. *Social Security Programs Throughout the World, 1987.* Washington, D.C.: U.S. Department of Health and Human Services.

Solon, Gary. 1992. "Intergenerational Income Mobility in the United States." *American Economic Review* 82 (3): 393–408.

Steiner, G. 1976. *The Children's Cause.* Washington, D.C.: Brookings Institute.

Stone, M. 1983. "Housing and the Economic Crisis." In *America's Housing Crisis: What Is to Be Done?,* ed. C. Hartman. Boston: Routledge and Kegan Paul.

Sulzbach, W. 1947. *German Experience with Social Insurance.* New York: National Industrial Conference Board.

Suter, L., and Miller, H. 1973. "Income Differences Between Men and Career Women." *American Journal of Sociology* 78 (January): 962–974.

Sweet, J.A. 1972. "The Living Arrangements of Separated, Widowed, and Divorced Mothers." *Demography* 9 (February): 143–157.

Sweet, J.A., and Bumpass, L. 1987. *American Families and Households.* New York: Russell Sage Foundation.

Testa, M. 1991. "Male Joblessness, Nonmarital Parenthood, and Marriage." Paper presented at the Urban Poverty and Family Life Conference, University of Chicago, October 10–12.

Thornton, C. 1989. "Costs of Welfare Programs." In *Welfare Policy for the 1990s,* ed. P.H. Cottingham and D.T. Ellwood. 247–268. Cambridge, Mass.: Harvard University Press.

Tienda, M. 1989. "Race, Ethnicity and the Portrait of Inequality: Approaching the 1990s." *Sociological Spectrum* 9:23–52.

Tobin, J. 1994. "Poverty in Relation to Macroeconomic Trends, Cycles, and Policies." In *Confronting Poverty: Prescriptions for Change,* ed. S. Danziger; G. Sandefur; and D. Weinberg. 147–167. Cambridge, Mass.: Harvard University Press.

Townsend, P. 1979. *Poverty in the United Kingdom.* Los Angeles: University of California Press.

Treiman, D., and Hauser, R. 1977. "Intergenerational Transmission of Income: An Exercise in Theory Construction." In *The Process of Stratification: Trends and Analyses,* ed. R.M. Hauser and D.L. Featherman. New York: Academic Press.

Treiman, D.J., and Hartmann, H.I., eds. 1981. *Women, Work, and Wages: Equal Pay for Jobs of Equal Value.* Washington, D.C.: National Academy Press.

U.S. Bureau of the Census. Various years (a). *Current Population Reports.* Series P-60. Washington, D.C.: GPO.

———. Various years (b). "Household and Family Characteristics. March of Each Year." *Current Population Reports.* Series P-20. Washington, D.C.: GPO.

———. 1985a. "Money Income and Poverty Status of Families and Persons in the United States: 1984." *Current Population Reports.* Series P-60, no. 149. Washington, D.C.: GPO.

———. 1985b. "Economic Characteristics of Households in the United States: First Quarter, 1984." *Current Population Reports.* Series P-70, no. 3. Washington, D.C.: GPO.

————. 1986. "Economic Characteristics of Households in the United States: Fourth Quarter, 1985." *Current Population Reports*. Series P-70, no. 6: 24–25. Washington, D.C.: GPO.

————. 1987. *Statistical Abstract of the United States 1988*. 108th ed. Washington, D.C.: GPO.

————. 1988. "Money Income and Poverty Status of Families and Persons in the United States: 1987." *Current Population Reports*. Series P-60, no. 161. Washington, D.C.: GPO.

————. 1989. *Statistical Abstract of the United States 1989*. 109th ed. Washington, D.C.: GPO.

————. 1991. "Family Disruption and Economic Hardship: The Short-Run Picture for Children." *Current Population Reports*. Series P-70, no. 23. Washington, D.C.: GPO.

————. 1992. "Fertility of American Women: June 1992." *Current Population Reports*. Series P-20, no. 470. Washington, D.C.: GPO.

————. 1993. "Poverty in the United States: 1992." *Current Population Reports*. Series P-60, no. 185. Washington, D.C.: GPO.

————. 1994a. *Statistical Abstract of the United States 1994*. 114th ed. Washington, D.C.: GPO.

————. 1994b. "Marital Status and Living Arrangements: March 1993." *Current Population Reports*. Series P-20, no. 478. Washington, D.C.: GPO.

————. 1995. "Income, Poverty, and Valuation of Noncash Benefits: 1993." *Current Population Reports*. Series P-60, no. 188. Washington, D.C.: GPO.

U.S. Congressional Budget Office. 1983. "Major Legislative Changes in Human Resource Programs Since January 1981." Staff memorandum.

U.S. Congressional Budget Office and National Commission for Employment Policy (NCEP). 1982. "CETA Training Programs—Do They Work for Adults?" Washington, D.C.: GPO.

U.S. General Accounting Office. 1980. *Better Management and More Resources Needed to Strengthen Federal Efforts to Improve Pregnancy Outcomes*. Washington, D.C.: GAO.

————. 1984. *CWEP's Implementation Results to Date Raise Questions About the Administration's Proposed Mandatory Work Program*. Report PEMD-84-2. Washington, D.C.: GAO.

————. 1987. *Work and Welfare: Current AFDC Work Programs and Implications for Federal Policy*. Report HRD-87-34. Washington, D.C.: GAO.

————. 1991. *Mother-Only Families: Low Earnings Will Keep Many Children in Poverty*. Report HRD-91-62. Washington, D.C.: GAO.

————. 1994a. *Families on Welfare: Sharp Rise in Never-Married Women Reflects Societal Trend*. Report HEHS-94-92. Washington, D.C.: GAO.

————. 1994b. *Families on Welfare: Teenage Mothers Least Likely to Become Self-Sufficient*. Report HEHS-94-115. Washington, D.C.: GAO.

————. 1994c. *Families on Welfare: Focus on Teenage Mothers Could Enhance Welfare Reform Efforts*. Report HEHS-94-112. Washington, D.C.: GAO.

————. 1994d. *Multiple Employment Training Programs: Major Overhaul Is Needed*. Washington, D.C.: GAO.

————. 1994e. *Welfare to Work: Current AFDC Program Is Not Sufficiently Focused on Employment.* Washington, D.C.: GAO.

U.S. House. 1983a. Select Committee on Children, Youth, and Families. *Children, Youth and Families: Beginning the Assessment.* 98th Cong., 1st Sess.

————. 1983b. Select Committee on Children, Youth, and Families. *U.S. Children and Their Families: 1983: Current Conditions and Recent Trends.* 98th Cong., 1st Sess.

————. 1984a. Select Committee on Children, Youth, and Families. *Demographic and Social Trends: Implications for Federal Support of Dependent-Care Service for Children and the Elderly.* 98th Cong., 1st Sess.

————. 1984b. Select Committee on Children, Youth, and Families. *Children, Youth and Families: 1983.* 98-117. 98th Cong., 2d Sess.

————. 1984c. Select Committee on Children, Youth, and Families. *Federal Programs Affecting Children.* 98th Cong., 1st Sess.

————. 1984d. Select Committee on Children, Youth, and Families. *Teenagers in Crisis: Issues and Programs.* 98th Cong.

————. 1985a. Committee on Ways and Means. *Children in Poverty.* 99th Cong., 1st Sess.

————. 1985b. Select Committee on Children, Youth, and Families. *Opportunities for Success: Cost Effective Programs for Children.* 99th Cong.

————. 1985c. Select Committee on Hunger. *The Effects of Hunger on Infant and Child Health in the U.S.* 99th Cong.

————. 1987a. Select Committee on Children, Youth, and Families. *Child Care: Key to Employment in a Changing Economy.* 100th Cong.

————. 1987b. Select Committee on Children, Youth, and Families. *Federal Programs Affecting Children, 1987.* 100th Cong.

————. 1988. Select Committee on Children, Youth, and Families. *American Families in Tomorrow's Economy.* 100th Cong.

————. 1993. Committee on Ways and Means. *Overview of Entitlement Programs. Green Book.* Washington, D.C.: GPO.

————. 1994. Committee on Ways and Means. *Overview of Entitlement Programs. Green Book.* Washington, D.C.: GPO.

U.S. Senate. 1980. Subcommittee on Public Assistance. *Statistical Data Reflected to Public Assistance Programs.* 96th Cong., 2d Sess.

Vincent, M.L.; Clearie, A.F.; and Schluchter, M.D. 1987. "Reducing Adolescent Pregnancy Through School and Community Based Education." *Journal of the American Medical Association* 257: 3382–3386.

Vining, D.R. 1983. "Illegitimacy and Public Policy." *Population and Development Review* 9 (March): 202–211.

Vinovskis, M.A. 1981. "An 'Epidemic' of Adolescent Pregnancy? Some Historical Considerations." *Journal of Family History* 6 (summer): 59–73.

Wagner, L.M., and Wagner, M. 1976. *The Danish National Child Care System.* Boulder, Colo.: Westview.

Walker, G. 1989. "Comment by Gary Walker." In *Welfare Policy for the 1990s,* ed. P.H. Cottingham and D.T. Ellwood. 141–145. Cambridge, Mass.: Harvard University Press.

Weatherley, R. 1985. "Adolescent Pregnancy: Patriarchy and the Politics of Transgression." Paper presented at the annual meeting of the Western Political Science Association, Las Vegas, Nevada.

———. 1988. "Teenage Parenthood and Poverty." In *Beyond Welfare: New Approaches to the Problem of Poverty in America,* ed. H.R. Rodgers Jr., 114–134. Armonk, N.Y.: M.E. Sharpe.

Weir, M.; Orloff, A.S.; and Skocpol, T., eds. 1988. *The Politics of Social Policy in the United States.* Princeton, N.J.: Princeton University Press.

Weitzman, L.J. 1980. "The Economics of Divorce: Social and Economic Consequences of Property, Alimony and Child Support Awards." *UCLA Law Review* 28:4–21.

Wellisch, C., et al. 1983. "The National Evaluation of School Nutrition Programs: Final Report." Santa Monica, Calif.: System Development Corporation 1 (April): 4–8.

Wilensky, H. 1975. *The Welfare State and Equality.* Berkeley: University of California Press.

Wilson, W.J. 1980. *The Declining Significance of Race,* 2d ed. Chicago: University of Chicago Press.

———. 1987. *The Truly Disadvantaged: The Inner City and Public Policy.* Chicago: University of Chicago Press.

Wilson, W., and Neckerman, K. 1986. "Poverty and Family Structure: The Widening Gap Between Evidence and Public Policy Issues." In *Fighting Poverty: What Works and What Doesn't,* ed. S. Danziger and D. Weinberg. Cambridge, Mass.: Harvard University Press.

Wiseman, M. 1988. "Workfare and Welfare Reform." In *Beyond Welfare: New Approaches to the Problem of Poverty in America,* ed. H.R. Rodgers Jr. 14–38. Armonk, N.Y.: M.E. Sharpe.

———. 1993. "Welfare Reform in the States: The Bush Legacy." *Focus* 15 (1): 18–36.

Wolf, W., and Fligstein, N. 1979. "Sex and Authority in the Workplace: Causes of Sexual Inequality." *American Sociological Review* 44 (April): 619–630.

Wolfe, B., and Hill, S. 1993. "The Health, Earnings Capacity, and Poverty of Single-Mother Families." In *Poverty and Prosperity in the USA in the Late Twentieth Century,* ed. D. Papadimitriou and E. Wolff. 89–120. New York: Macmillan.

Wong, Y.I.; Garfinkel, I.; and McLanahan, S. 1993. "Understanding Cross-national Variation in Occupational Mobility." *American Sociological Review* 55:560–573.

Yavis, J. 1982. "The Head Start Program—History, Legislation, Issues and Funding—1964–1982." Congressional Research Service Report no. 82-93 EPW (May).

Young, D.R., and Nelson, R.R., eds. 1973. *Public Policy for Day Care of Young Children.* Lexington, Mass.: Lexington Books.

Young, K.T., and Zigler, E. 1986. "Infant and Toddler Day Care: Regulations and Policy Implications." *American Journal of Orthopsychiatry* 56:43–55.

Zabin, L.S.; Hirsch, M.B.; Smith, E.A.; Streett, R.; and Hardy, J.B. 1986.

"Evaluation of a Pregnancy Prevention Program for Urban Teenagers." *Family Planning Perspectives* 18: 119–126.

Zabin, L.S.; Hirsch, M.B.; Streett, R.; Emerson, M.R.; Smith, M.; Hardy, J.B.; and King, T.M. 1988. "The Baltimore Pregnancy Prevention Program for Urban Teenagers: How Did It Work?" *Family Planning Perspectives* 20: 182–187.

Zelnik, M., and Kanter, J.F. 1980. "Sexual Activity, Contraceptive Use and Pregnancy Among Metropolitan-Area Teenagers." *Family Planning Perspectives* 12 (September–October): 111–127.

Zelnik, M.; Kanter, J.F.; and Ford, K. 1981. *Sex and Pregnancy in Adolescence.* Beverly Hills, Calif.: Sage.

Index

Acs, G., 62
Advance maintenance payments, 118–119, 128
AFDC. *See* Aid to Families with Dependent Children
Age
 of first marriage, 53
 out-of-wedlock births and, 58
 poverty rate and, 28–30
 of working women (mean), 66
Aid to Dependent Children (ADC), 71
Aid to Families with Dependent Children (AFDC)
 child care, 99–100, 133, 134, 136
 child support enforcement and, 93, 94, 132, 167–168
 decline in benefits, 67, 91–92
 earnings of mothers, 97–99, 133
 employment of mothers, 97–99
 family size and, 86
 income disregards in, 87, 96, 97
 job programs, 95–96, 96–97, 100, 131, 132–133, 134–135, 136, 150–152
 long- and short-term users, 94–95, 100
 Medicaid coverage, 92, 133, 136
 mother-only families and, 86–87
 origins of, 71
 out-of-wedlock birth rate and, 62–63
 poverty rate and, 21–22, 66–67, 106–107
 problems with, 100–101
 reasons for exits, 95
 reduction in benefits, 82

spending on, 76, 77, 83–86
teenage mothers and, 101, 136
unemployed parents (UP) program, 74, 75, 83, 133–134, 151
variations in benefits, 72, 74, 87–92
WIC program, 105
Alcohol addiction, relation to child poverty, 21
American Medical Association, 72
At-Risk Child Care programs, 99
Australia, poverty rate in, 108
Austria
 child support in, 118
 health expenditures in, 125
 poverty rate in, 108

Bane, M.J., 21, 53, 61, 62, 94, 95
Bassi, L., 61
Beckerman, W., 108
Behn, R.D., 154
Belgium
 family allowance in, 115
 health expenditures in, 125
Bergman, B., 66
Berrueta-Clement, J.R., 102, 103
Birthrate
 family allowance and, 116
 out-of-wedlock, 8, 52–53, 62
Bishop, J., 149
Black mother-only families
 child poverty in, 46, 48

195

About the Author

Harrell R. Rodgers, Jr., is professor of political science at the University of Houston. He has published widely on poverty and social welfare programs in the United States, Western Europe, and developing nations and is a past winner of the Aaron Wildavsky book prize and a *Choice* Outstanding Academic Book award.